The Family Garden Plan

Melissa K. Norris

HARVEST HOUSE PUBLISHERS
EUGENE, OREGON

❧ Contents ❧

Introduction

Growing a garden is as much food for the soul as it is for the body. There is little more satisfying, or delicious, than walking out your backdoor and picking a fresh, vine-ripened tomato or filling a colander full of carrots and beets with soil still lingering on the roots.

Watching the cycle of a garden, from the dormant earth, first seed sprouting, producing the harvest, and then gifting us with another seed to perform the cycle again, is like witnessing a small miracle each year. My heart is filled with a gratefulness for the way the good Lord created this earth and the food to nourish our bodies that I don't find in the same depth when purchasing off the store shelf.

After all, God is the Creator—this world and the very depth of nature we see before us is His canvas and design. Watching it up close, how the chill of winter is necessary for production of fruit and some seeds to sprout, to the rains of spring so those seeds can germinate, and the summer warmth to bring everything to fruition and harvest, is a testimony to His hand.

Yet there are springs when the rains aren't bountiful, the sun is scorching, and plants die; and it's in these times perhaps I'm more appreciative of the harvest I get, knowing even when the earth doesn't work with me the way I'd like, God will provide and teach me as I go.

It used to be almost every household had at the very least a small kitchen garden where they grew some of their own food. In much of today's mainstream society we've traded our connection to our food and land for the convenience of having someone else grow it for us. But you and I, my friend (because I consider all other gardeners friends), we know the importance and joy of

raising nourishing and healthy food for ourselves and our family that goes well beyond the plate and pocketbook.

I've found gardening to be one of the simplest and most complex things there is. It really is as simple as plopping a seed into the soil, providing some sunlight and water, and letting it grow. But on the other hand, the condition of the soil, growing zones, pest management, and any number of other things come into play in determining whether that plant will thrive and provide you with a bountiful harvest.

I come from a long line of gardeners. Some of my earliest memories are of springs filled with planting the garden, snapping beans alongside my father, and filling up the jars for the pressure canner alongside my mother. I hail from people who made their living from the land; and if they didn't raise or grow it themselves, they would have gone hungry.

My husband and I, along with our two children, raise all our own meat and over half of our fruits and vegetables for the year on 14.96 acres here in the foothills of the North Cascade mountain range of Washington State. As we strive to increase what we grow and preserve each year, we've learned a lot—more from the failures than the successes, though thankfully we have more successes now than when we first started some 19 years ago.

No matter how many times I've grown the same crop or raised a garden, I learn something new every year and season. A garden will teach you many lessons, and only some of them are about food. It is my aim with this book to walk you through what I've been blessed to learn, what other gardeners who have gone before me have shared, and to help you raise just a little bit more of your own food than you did the year before.

I don't believe it's possible for one book to cover every area of gardening; exhausting every facet of composting, permaculture, and seed saving are all separate books. But I will cover what you need to know to have a solid foundation to raise your own fruits, vegetables, and herbs from planning and planting to harvesting; I'll give you tips to implement and extra resources should you need to dive in deeper than we will in these pages. Deal? Good. Let the growing begin!

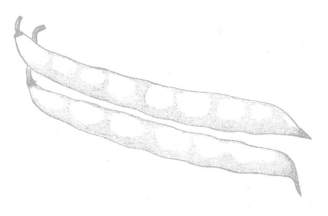

Planning Your Food Crops

~ ONE ~

Planning Your Food Crops

Commit to the LORD whatever you do,
and he will establish your plans.

PROVERBS 16:3

A customized plan based on your family's needs, space, and gardening zone is one of the often most overlooked but critical steps to a successful growing season and harvest. One of the biggest mistakes we made in our early years of homesteading, my husband and I both agree, is that we didn't keep the best of records when we started out.

The small amount of planning done now will guide you throughout your entire year of gardening and ensure you're raising food and crops your family will put to good use. Because, let's face it—it doesn't matter if we have a huge garden if it's full of foods our family doesn't like and we're not eating.

Whether this is your first year or you're a gardening veteran, planning will serve you well. We do this every winter as we gear up for the growing season.

No one garden is the same, nor should it be. Your garden will evolve and change every year, a living canvas for the gardener to erase his mistakes and hone his talent. You'll find my planning very practical. I believe in planting what my family enjoys and eats the most (alas, I've not found a chocolate plant that will grow here—but raspberries are a close second) and can be preserved to stock our pantry for the off-season.

CREATING A CUSTOMIZED GARDEN PLAN

No matter if you've been planting and preserving for years or this is your first year, we'll start by going to our cupboards and freezers.

Look at your current pantry and freezer and take note of which foods you eat on a regular basis. Keep track of the meals and foods you're consuming regularly. If you use a written meal plan, this is already done for you.

Do you have spaghetti, chili, or something with tomato sauce in it weekly? What frozen or canned vegetables are you using on a consistent basis? Don't forget the spice and herb cupboard.

Document this, write it all down, and keep a record of what you'd use in an average month. Then multiply out for a year. Use the Food Needs for a Year Worksheet at the end of this chapter to help you do so. This step lets you know what and how much to plant for the current year's gardens.

Example from My Kitchen

When I went through this process, I found in January that I had 18 jars of tomato sauce left. Our typical first large harvest of tomatoes (enough to make sauce) isn't until August. I can use approximately two jars a month if I don't want to purchase any from the store. This past year I tried a new type of tomatoes and didn't grow as many paste tomato plants as I usually do. I made a note to go back to 20 plants of San Marzano Lungo 2.

With 27 jars of cucumber pickles left, at a jar a week until main harvest time, we have plenty (we generally don't eat an entire quart of pickles in one week). This means having three hills (nine plants) of pickling cucumbers is the perfect amount for our current needs.

I go through this process with all my preserved foods, including dehydrated, canned, and frozen food.

Using the Food Needs for a Year Worksheet, evaluate how much food you have left from last year's garden or how much you need to feed your family for a year of each crop. Now it's time to plan what crops and how much of them you'll be planting for your family's needs. It's important to note: this will likely change every year.

One year I had 30 jars of salsa left over. I didn't can any salsa that year; instead, I used up what we had. Some years I preserve a double amount of a crop and skip growing it the following year. Best practice is to use home-canned goods in 12 to 18 months.

It's crucial that you go through your inventory each year and not run on autopilot. Right now, my son is hitting his teenage years (aka eating a lot more food). My daughter loves pickles (she didn't use to). Over the years, we eat more of some things or less; and the beauty and point of growing your own food is that you can tailor your harvest to your exact needs.

YOUR GROWING SEASON

Gardening zones and first and last frost dates will determine what you can grow and when to plant it. Basically, your entire gardening season depends upon these dates.

To search online for your gardening zone information, type into the search bar your zip code, city, and state with the words *average first and last frost date* and *gardening zone*. It's also wise to ask an experienced gardener in your area if possible.

With the widespread use of social media, you can even find gardening groups online in your specific area. These can be goldmines of information, especially when it comes to microzones and microclimates.

Your gardening zone allows you to know which plants will grow and thrive in that specific location. The USDA hardiness map divides North America into zones based on the average annual minimal winter temperature using 10-degree Fahrenheit increments. You can access the map at https://planthardiness.ars.usda.gov/PHZMWeb/.

After identifying your gardening zone and first and last frost date, you'll want to look at microzones.

What Is a Microzone?

Microzones are smaller growing zones within your large gardening zone based on the USDA hardiness guidelines. For example, according to multiple sources, I am the larger gardening zone 8a, with a last average frost date (when I can safely plant warm-weather plants in the spring) of April 8 and first average frost date of November 3.

This information supposedly applies to our whole county, but because I've lived and gardened on this same stretch of land my entire life, I know this isn't true. If you drive toward the ocean an hour away from us, you'll find the information fairly accurate; but we live in the foothills of the Cascades and sometimes experience extreme winter low temperatures for a week or two that would put us much closer to gardening zone 6 for frost dates and average winter temps of 7b.

The first average hard frost date for us (a killing frost that wipes out your warm-weather crops) is usually the first part of October. We can experience light frosts as early as the middle to end of September.

We've also had frost as late as May 1 and never plant our warm-weather crops until mid-May, sometimes as late as Memorial Day weekend. This is about two to three weeks later than our neighbors down the mountain and lower in the valley.

This gives us about a 150-day growing season for warm-weather crops between the frost dates. You can see why it's important to take note of frosts in your area, talk to longtime gardeners, and use the online information as your guideline. Record your gardening zone, frost dates, and growing season in the Growing Season Worksheet at the end of the chapter.

Armed with this information, you can begin to select which plants will grow in your area and which varieties to plant. When viewing seed packets, you'll often see an indication of 50 days or 120 days to harvest. This is the number of days from sowing the seed until it produces a harvest.

When you know how many days are in your growing season, you can better select varieties that are suited to your area and time frame.

Don't waste your time trying to baby plants that aren't adapted to your growing climate and season. I live in the Pacific Northwest, where it's too cold to grow okra and sweet potatoes. Could I try with a large black grow bag or using solarization methods of clear plastic to heat up the soil? Yes, maybe someday—but it would take a lot of babying and extra work on my part without a high likelihood of a large crop if we have a rainy, cool stretch during the summer months. For this reason, it's very low on my gardening priority list. In the same vein, if you live in a hot climate, you're probably not going to have luck with snow peas and spinach; they like cooler weather.

Using the list of foods you and your family eat often (see page 24), see which plants won't grow in your gardening zone and cross them off.

Below you will find lists of crops that do best in warm weather (intolerant of frosts) and cool weather (handles frosts).

If you live in southern hot climates, avoid some of the cool-weather crops; many of them won't germinate, bolt quickly (stop growing, turn bitter, and immediately go to seed), or won't produce fruit if temps get above 75 degrees Fahrenheit. You may try them in winter depending on your average temperatures.

If you live in northern climates, you may have trouble growing some of the warmer crops even in the summer months if you don't use a hoop house or other coverings on cooler nights.

That said, there are usually some workarounds that will allow you to grow most of the crops you wish, which we'll discuss next.

Cool-Weather Crops

Will Tolerate Cooler Daytime and Nighttime Temps but Don't Handle Hard Frosts

cauliflower	celery	lettuce	potatoes

Will Tolerate Frosts

beets	carrots	leeks	peas
bok choy	chard	lettuce (cold-hardy	radishes
broccoli	garlic	leaf varieties are best)	rutabaga
brussels sprouts	kale	onions	spinach
cabbage	kohlrabi	parsnip	turnips

Warm-Weather Crops

beans

corn

cucumber

eggplant

herbs (basil, cilantro, dill, German chamomile, nasturtium, parsley, stevia)

melons

okra (does best with warm days and nights; cool temps result in low to no yield)

peppers

pumpkins

sweet potatoes (Soil temperature needs to be at 80 to 90+ degrees Fahrenheit. You can do this in
northern climates, but it requires using solarization to heat the soil and enough hot days throughout the
summer for growth and harvest.)

summer squash (zucchini, pattypan, crookneck, etc.)

tomatillos

tomatoes

winter squash (acorn, butternut, Hubbard, spaghetti, etc.)

Microclimates

A whatta climate? So glad you asked. Microclimates exist naturally on your property, and you can even create or enhance them for your crop needs. They work very well when you may have a borderline growing environment for a specific plant.

Almost all yards or houses have four particular areas.

Southern exposure areas on your property or in your yard, especially tucked up near a house or shed, get hotter than any other spot on your property. If you're in a cooler climate, this is an ideal place to grow some of those heat-loving plants. When my rosemary plant was in the main garden area, it died every single winter; but when I put it in a large, black pot and nestled it against our back deck, smack-dab in the middle of our southern exposure, it's survived every winter and is now going on five years old. Behold, the power of microclimates.

Eastern exposure receives the first light of morning, but usually moves into the shade come midday. This is perfect for plants that don't like to get too hot and tolerate some shade. I planted my sage in our eastern-exposure area and it flourishes.

Western exposure usually gets the afternoon sun all the way through to sunset. This is great for plants that require a lot of sunlight and tolerate the high heat of midday sun.

Northern exposure is best for plants that don't like to get hot and can tolerate quite a bit of shade. Most vegetables require six or more hours of sunlight, so be careful if you have deep shade in your northern areas. We don't grow any of our vegetables or fruit in northern exposure with the exception of blackberries; we have invasive varieties that have been deemed noxious weeds by our county, and they don't seem to be deterred by full shade.

Other microclimates occur in natural hills, slopes, and valleys on your property. Some plants need more water and will grow better at the bottom of a slope or in a dip where water will naturally funnel. But other plants don't like wet feet and will not do well here.

On our property, the bottom of the hill is naturally protected from high winds. It receives more water, which helps in summer when water is scarce. But during the rainy season (here in the Pacific Northwest this would be pretty much mid-September through June), it can become water-logged if the soil isn't draining well.

Rocky areas, especially with larger rocks or cement, will naturally soak up the heat from the sun and radiate it. This is best for drought-tolerant and heat-loving plants. Our lavender and oregano do quite well in these spots. We also grow our grapes over the top of our cement patio.

Wind breaks create a protective block from winds that can damage plants. We live in a valley, and during the winter freezing winds funnel down from the Frasier River Valley in Canada when conditions are right (the old-timers here say, "The northeastern is blowing") and blow frigid gusts across our top pasture. We have a natural wind break from the trees in front of our house, but the top pasture is wide open. Where the hill drops down to the bottom pasture, it blocks the wind. This is important for protecting younger trees and tender plants.

If you have a windy area in your yard or property, you can create wind blocks with a building, other plants and trees (make sure you choose evergreen types so you have year-round protection), or even large rocks.

Take note of the natural microclimates on your property to optimize your planting locations, and add manmade variations if needed.

My Microclimates

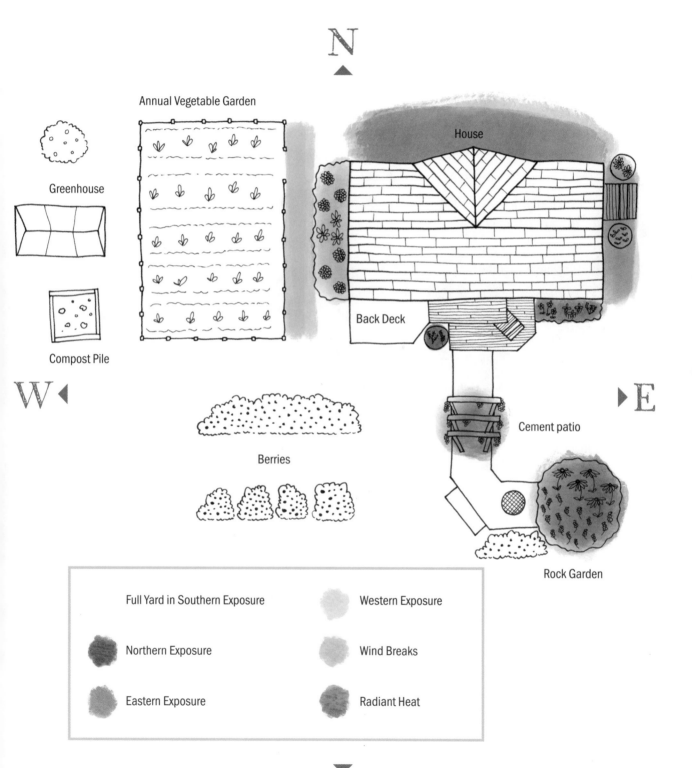

N

Annual Vegetable Garden

Greenhouse

Compost Pile

House

Back Deck

Cement patio

W

E

Berries

Rock Garden

Full Yard in Southern Exposure

Western Exposure

Northern Exposure

Wind Breaks

Eastern Exposure

Radiant Heat

S

Season Extenders

Even though cold temps dictate our planting and harvesting, the use of season extenders can provide extra weeks or months of growing and harvest time.

Season extenders are used in the spring and the fall. Our high tunnel (unheated greenhouse) gives at least four weeks of additional growing time. I can plant two weeks earlier in the spring and keep my tomatoes protected from frost by at least two weeks in the fall. In the winter, I'm able to grow lettuce almost all season long.

There are many other options that don't include a greenhouse or building.

Frost cloth, sheets, or blankets work best for cool-weather plants. If applied correctly (staked to the ground to trap heat) they will protect plants down to 30 or 20 degrees Fahrenheit.[1]

Cold frames use a window on top of an open box, usually made of wood or straw bales, to create a greenhouse effect.

Hoop houses or mini tunnels use greenhouse plastic or row cover to insulate plants underneath.

Individual covers in glass or plastic (cloches): place a milk jug (top cut off) or glass jar upside down over top of the plant at night, and remove in the morning.

No matter which season extender option you choose, remember you need to monitor temperatures—remove or open them when temps are warm and close them when temps are cold.

FOOD NEEDS FOR A YEAR WORKSHEET

Here is a worksheet to help you document and plan out approximate yearly needs based on your family's eating habits. This will help you both during the growing season for fresh eating per week and also with your food preservation for the pantry shelf.

Individual Fruits/Vegetables

Food	Serving Amount Per Meal	Week 1	Week 2	Week 3	Week 4	Weekly Average	Yearly Need
	2 cups, 1 pound, etc.	Serving amount x meals	Serving amount x meals	Serving amount x meals	Serving amount x meals	Total serving amounts divided by 4 weeks	Average weekly use x 52 weeks
green beans	2 cups	2x2= 4 cups	2x0= 0 cups	2x1= 2 cups	2x0= 0 cups	6 cups/ 4 weeks= 1 1/2 cups	1 1/2 cups x 52 weeks = 78 cups

Combination Recipes

Food	Serving Amount Per Meal	Week 1	Week 2	Week 3	Week 4	Weekly Average	Yearly Need
salsa	1 cup	1x1 = 1 cup	1x0 = 0 cups	1x1 = 1 cup	1x2 = 2 cups	4 cups/ 4 weeks= 1 cup	1 cup x 52 weeks = 52 cups

GROWING SEASON WORKSHEET

1. My gardening zone is _____.

2. My last average frost date is _____.

3. My first average frost date is _____.

4. My growing season is_____ days.

CROP PLANNING WORKSHEET

Now that you know which foods your family is eating a lot of, it's time to decide which of these crops you'll be planting in your garden this year.

When deciding what plants to grow, consider:

- Your growing season (refer to crops by cool or warm season on pages 16,18). For example, even though we use on average a lime a week, citrus doesn't grow in our gardening zone, so we don't grow it.

- What grows easily in your area.

Annual Vegetables	Perennial Vegetables	Fruit	Herbs
zucchini	asparagus	raspberries	rosemary

MICROCLIMATE WORKSHEET

Evaluate your yard, property, and house, and identify your existing microclimates. Write down any areas where you wish to create a microclimate. In cooler climates take advantage of southern exposure areas, especially when up against a wall, rocks, or cement areas that retain and release the heat from the day during the night hours for heat-loving crops like basil and rosemary during the winter.

Existing Microclimate	Crop
Southern Exposure	*berries*

SEASON EXTENDER WORKSHEET

What season extenders do you plan to use for which crops?

Example: I use our greenhouse for tomatoes and peppers. The sheltered herb pots tucked up against the house allow me to harvest perennial herbs almost year-round. The house provides a wind break for the annual vegetable garden without blocking the sun and allows us to grow and harvest kale ten months out of the year. I use plastic cloches (reused milk jugs and produce clam shells) for winter sowing and greens.

Season Extender	Crop
greenhouse	*tomatoes, peppers*

Planning
Your
Garden
Space

Planning Your Garden Space

Plans fail for lack of counsel,
but with many advisers they succeed.

Proverbs 15:22

Taking the time to plan out your garden will save you a lot of angst and bring you baskets of bountiful harvest that much faster. I confess I've not always been a planner, but I've learned the hard way to spend some planning time up front to save myself (and my poor plants) later down the growing season.

WORK WITH THE GROWING SPACE YOU HAVE

It's important to work with what we've got. We'll cover more on soil improvement later; but for now, let's focus on space in relation to your crops.

When choosing where to place your garden or plants, consider these key things.

Sunlight

Most of your fruits and vegetables require at least six hours of full sunlight a day for ideal growth. One mistake we made was planting our fruit trees in late winter when the maple trees didn't have their leaves. Come summer, the leaves from the maples blocked the sun and we had to move the trees to a different area of the yard the following year. This stunted our fruit production by a full year due to recovery time after transplanting.

Look at any buildings or tall trees and make sure they won't be blocking the sun come summer time.

If you live in a really hot climate, consider areas offering early morning sun while providing some afternoon shade for less heat-tolerant plants.

Water Source

Even here in the notoriously rainy Pacific Northwest, we still water our annual vegetable garden in the dead of summer. When picking your gardening spot, make sure you have easy water access. If using hoses, the farther away you are from the spigot, the more hose you'll need to purchase. Keep in mind you will experience a decrease in water pressure at the end of the run. If watering by hand, it will take more time—and while you'll gain more muscles from packing the water, you might decide you'd rather gain muscle in ways other than lugging gallons of water to your plants.

Runoff and Slopes

Remember your microclimates? If you plant your vegetable garden at the bottom of a slope, most of the water (from a sprinkler, soaker hose, or rain) will run off and collect at the bottom.

It's also important to look at the property adjoining yours. Will anything from your neighbor's land flow onto yours? If your neighbor sprays weed killer, is their property sloped toward your vegetable garden? Will it naturally flow and contaminate it?

Next time you have a good rainfall, take a few minutes outside and watch where puddles form and identify any runoff areas.

Are you next to a busy roadway? Plants here are exposed to runoff and vehicle pollutants.

Available Space

Maximize the available space you have. I know this sounds basic, but it's often overlooked. This involves choosing appropriate crops and varieties.

An easy example of this is pole beans. I find pole beans are more prolific (a larger harvest from the same amount of plants) than bush beans. They're less susceptible to mildew and mold. I plant our pole beans near our squash so it can vine out among the beans, letting me use the space for two crops at the same time.

Some crops require more space due to their pollination. Corn is one of these crops; it does best when planted in a square with multiples of at least four rows deep, instead of in one single line.

Take a small amount of time to understand the growing conditions and preferences of each crop and make sure you're placing them in the best spot with the space you have.

Vertical gardening helps you maximize your space and can help eliminate some pest and disease issues.

GROWING CROPS VERTICALLY

Growing plants vertically has many advantages, including more food with the same amount of square footage and an easier harvest because you're not bent over the whole time and can see the produce better. Plus, it provides better air flow, resulting in less powdery mildew or fungal disease.

Not all crops are suited for vertical growing. Some people will refer to vertical growing by simply meaning a plant is in a container and not directly in the ground, but that's not what I'm talking about. We'll go over container and raised-bed gardening shortly.

Vertical gardening is when you put the plant directly in the ground and provide support for it to climb, allowing the leaves, vines, and eventually produce to suspend from the trellis in the air, not down on the ground.

I prefer to put the support system in first and then plant around it. Not only does this save time because I don't plant and have to go back later to put in the support system, but it also ensures I don't damage the root system of the plant when doing so and that I can position the plants exactly as I want around the base.

Vertical Support Options

This is where your creativity comes into play. Anything tall and stable enough to support the weight of the plant can be used. Below are several common options.

A-frame. Usually a wooden frame with either wire or wooden slats for plants to climb.

Arbor. A wooden arbor over a walkway or covering a back patio or deck is the perfect structure for more than just climbing roses and wisteria (though both are lovely). We have grapes on our arbor, which provides us with shade in the heat of summer and lovely grapes come late summer and early fall.

Fence. A simple fence can provide support for vining plants. We prefer to use two- or three-inch square fencing wire between the poles. Chicken wire isn't a heavy enough gauge.

Pole and twine. We use this method for our raspberries and tomatoes. We've also used it for our pole beans in the past. Place a pole at the end of each row, with a few smaller support poles at the halfway point if row is longer than six feet. Then string a single strand of wire or twine between the poles and tie the plant to the guide wires using twine.

Teepee. Our preferred method for pole beans. We pound a center six-foot metal fence post into the ground and arrange three six-foot wooden split-cedar poles in a teepee around it, using wire at the top to secure them to the center pole. We plant the beans at the base of all three teepee poles as well as the center pole. You can try this without the center pole if you can pound your teepee poles deeper into the soil; but without the center pole, the weight of the beans, once mature, may cause your teepee to topple in high winds.

Trellis. Usually an open framework made with wood or metal, a trellis may be put against walls or pounded into the ground independently.

Wire. Bend heavy-gauge wire into an arbor or even a large circle and train vines to travel up the wire.

Best Vertical Crops

grapes

hardy kiwis

melons

peas

pole beans

tomatoes (The best types for vertical growing are indeterminate varieties that will grow and produce until first frost, some reaching upwards of ten feet, though ours usually get about six feet. Determinate varieties reach about three to four feet tall and are bushy rather than sprawling.)

summer squash (cucumbers, pattypan, zucchini)

winter squash (butternut, acorn, pumpkin)

Depending upon the size of the fruit or vegetable and the height of your trellis system, you may find you need to use a sling to support the fruit while it ripens on the vine. This is usually done with larger winter squash and melon varieties; small summer and winter squash shouldn't need this method. You can use any breathable material such as netting or mesh to create a sling. Think of creating a hammock for the fruit to sit in. You'll need to secure the end of the sling to the trellis support you're using, so make sure it's sturdy enough to hold the weight.

RAISED BEDS

Many people have fallen in love with raised-bed gardening. Raised beds can be beneficial in certain gardens, but I don't believe they're necessary across the board. When I talk about raised beds, I'm referring to a plot where the soil is above ground level (usually a minimum of 12 inches) with side walls. Sometimes people refer to large containers as raised beds; but in this book, I'm referring to a raised bed as elevated soil (no bottom).

Raised garden beds have both pros and cons, and I want you to make the best decision based on your gardening needs.

Reasons to Use Raised Beds

Pros

- Contaminated, compacted, poor draining soil (especially clay based). Raised beds allow you to bring in top soil and compost, creating better drainage and soil immediately, especially with rocky or poor draining areas. Soil in a raised bed isn't stepped on, so soil compaction is avoided, improving long-term drainage.

- PH level. Soil in a raised bed is easier to isolate and maintain (for more on pH levels see Soil Testing and Amending starting on page 197).

- Physical impairments or disabilities. Unable to bend down or over? Raised beds make it easier for people with disabilities or who have difficulty bending and kneeling, provided the beds are raised high enough to avoid stooping.

- Neat and orderly. If you have an engineer's mind or need things in neat and tidy spaces, you may prefer raised beds with dedicated pathways between them.

- Drainage. If you have a low area where water collects but is an otherwise ideal growing location, a raised bed can allow you to use that area while keeping plants and roots from drowning.

Cons

- Expense. You'll need to purchase soil and/or compost in large quantities for beds, retaining wall supplies if needed based on depth of the beds (usually metal or wood), and nails or screws to hold it together.

- Soil heat. While this may be considered a pro early in the spring, it's usually a con during summer or in hot climates.

- More water is needed. Due to higher temps above ground, raised beds use more water. To help avoid this, mulch in spring after planting and again in the fall to improve soil and improve moisture retention.

- Maintenance. Depending on your material choice, you may need to replace support walls. I found raised beds did not cut down on weeds long term. Initially, when you bring in weed-free soil, weed presence is diminished; but over time there is no difference in weed amount. I found it harder to maintain our raised bed when trying to use a hoe for weeding, due to the increased height (we were three feet deep and too wide to reach the middle from the side) and impossible to use our tiller for light shredding of organic material. This was partially due to not constructing it with an ideal width (heed my warning below).

If you decide a raised bed is for you, make sure you can reach the middle of each bed without having to step on or enter the bed. If you make the bed too wide, you'll have to crawl over and potentially damage crops to reach the middle of the bed when weeding and harvesting. A good rule of thumb is to make the bed three to four feet wide, allowing you to reach the middle of the bed from both sides, depending on your height and arm length. If in doubt, a three-foot width is best.

Raised Bed Depth

The depth you choose depends on the crops you plan to plant. Remember, if a plant is root-bound or can't develop its root system, it won't grow or produce as large a harvest.

If possible, a depth of two to three feet is ideal, though 12 inches will work for proper root room and drainage. If your bed is over six inches (which I highly recommend), you'll likely need walls and or a support system to keep the soil from eroding and spilling out.

Support and Wall Options

What materials do you already have? Larger rocks make excellent walls because they never break down or need replacing. They also retain warmth, which is good in cooler climates and early spring but not necessarily a good thing in droughts or the heat of summer.

Rot-resistant lumber, such as cedar or redwood, is also a good choice. I have heard cedar may be toxic to plants, but research from Washington State University says this is a myth. Linda Chalker-Scott, PhD, extension horticulturist and associate professor at the Puyallup Research and Extension Center of Washington State University says, "There is virtually no documented evidence for allelopathic activity in either Thuja or Cedrus spp."[1] In simpler words, there's no documented evidence that cedar bark releases chemicals that harm other plants.

Avoid pressure-treated lumber, especially when treated with creosote.

Other alternatives are brick and cinder blocks. Some people are concerned that chemicals from concrete, especially cinder blocks containing fly ash, may leech into the soil. I was unable to find any scientific studies regarding this one way or the other. If you decide to use cinder blocks, you can use a liner. Line the sides of the wall where the soil would be touching the blocks with a BPA-free, six-millimeter plastic liner, making sure you only line the walls and not the ground, for proper drainage.

CONTAINER GARDENING

Container gardening is exactly as it sounds: you grow plants inside containers. Most of us are familiar with flower pots; but truly, any container large enough to sustain the plant may be used.

Container gardens also have pros and cons, like any method, but they're an excellent addition, especially with limited space. Container gardening shines on patio and back deck gardens, but it can also be used in conjunction with larger gardens and acreage. We use container gardening for many of our herbs and pepper plants. You can grow anything in a container that you would in the ground, provided your container is large enough.

Container gardening is excellent for making the most of a microclimate, controlling invasive plants that you don't want to spread, or areas with poor soil or lack of soil. I like to plant my hot peppers in containers so I can move them in out of the rain and give them the full advantage of our southern exposure back deck heat. Whether you're able to move a container is going to depend on the size, but the container solution can work well for plants that are finicky or not ideal for your climate.

There are a plethora of container options available:

- plastic pots
- 5-gallon buckets (one of the easiest in both size and availability)
- grow bags (These come in sizes of 1, 2, 3, 5, 7, 10, 15, 20, 25, and 100 gallons. If storage is an issue, grow bags can be folded down during the off season. Remember, the larger bags are harder to remove and replace soil. Make sure large bags are in a permanent spot.)
- terra-cotta/clay pots
- glazed clay pots
- metal or tin pots
- repurposed items (Get creative! Think old rubber boots, watering cans, sinks and tubs, storage bins, garbage cans, old wheel barrows, pails—anything that will hold soil and you can put a few drain holes in.)

Proper Size

One of the biggest restraints with container gardening is the size. Some plants require more growing space than others. Tomatoes have a large root system, and root plants (beets, carrots, garlic, onion, turnips, parsnips, etc.) will be stunted if they don't have enough soil to grow.

Remember, the smaller the pot, the faster it dries out. Consider the container material. Terra-cotta, ceramic, and clay pots are beautiful natural material, but because they are porous the soil will dry out faster.

Drainage holes are a must. Plant roots don't like to sit in stagnant water. Most flower pots come with a drain hole in them, but if you're using other containers, like half whiskey barrels or buckets, you'll want to drill some drain holes in the bottom. For larger containers like a half whiskey barrel, I recommend several small drain holes.

The Washington State University Master Gardener program recommends these size guidelines for vegetables, and I've added several of my own from our container vegetable gardening.[2]

Container Size for Vegetables

6-inch or 1-gallon pot	1 lettuce or chard plant; 6–8 radishes or green onions; 3 spinach plants, or chives, parsley, or dill. Truth be told, I've grown a single jalapeno in a 1-gallon pot. I didn't get as many peppers, but it worked.
2-gallon pot	1 pepper plant; 1 cucumber
5-gallon bucket	1 tomato or zucchini; 2 peppers; 3–5 bush beans; 3–4 lettuces; 1 cabbage or broccoli (with 15 radishes or 8 spinach plants); 10 to 15 carrots or beets (my favorite carrot is Danvers Half Long); 6 bulb onions, garlic, or leeks; 8 mustards or turnips for greens.
Half whiskey barrel	10–12 lettuces; 6–9 bean plants; 60 radishes or green onions; 50 carrots or beets; 3 broccolis or cabbages (with several spinach plants); a whole salad: 4 lettuce, 1 cherry tomato, 8 carrots, 12 radishes, and 12 green onions.

Planting in Containers

With containers you'll be packing more plants into a smaller space. The general guideline is to follow the recommended space between plants and ignore row spacing. For example: radishes should be 1 inch apart with 12 inches between rows. In a container, you'd ignore the 12 inches and plant all your radishes 1 inch apart.

Make sure the container is deep enough to accommodate the roots of the vegetables you're putting in.

Soil for Container Planting

A container is a different environment than in-ground gardening or raised beds, where normal gravitational pressure forces the water through the soil. In a container, when the water gets to the bottom of the soil, there is no more dry soil (as in the earth) for it to travel to. This means soil in a container will end up holding more water than soil in the ground, and becomes saturated faster. That's why soil choice is important in containers.

It's a common myth (I even thought it true myself for years) that putting a layer of gravel in the bottom of a container will help with drainage. But it's the size of the soil and its absorption rate that affect your drainage; adding gravel or rocks to the bottom of the pot does nothing for the rate of time it takes the water to move through the soil, but it does take up pot space and give your roots less room.[3]

Instead, consider your potting mix, aka soil, carefully for containers. Due to gravitational and matric potential, you don't want to use your regular garden soil. Your soil needs good air-filled porosity and water-holding capacity, which refers to the air and water the soil holds after watering.

The most common potting mixes use coarse sand, peat moss, sawdust, vermiculite, and perlite. You can purchase potting mixes or even the individual ingredients to make your own. Pennsylvania State University recommends a homemade mixture of equal parts with one gallon of each sterilized loam soil, moist course sphagnum peat moss, followed by coarse sand, perlite, or vermiculite.[4]

Fertilizing

Containers are limited in the space of the soil and the nutrients available for plants. Even larger containers are still limited in comparison to raised beds or in-ground garden beds. Plus, in containers we often plant more plants per square foot of soil than we would in a regular garden bed. This means you need to provide outside nutrients to your plants by way of fertilizing.

You've probably guessed by now that I only use organic fertilizers. For perennials, begin applying fertilizer when plants show new growth and begin to bud. With annuals, apply fertilizer two to three weeks after planting.

I apply a fresh layer of organic compost to the top two to three inches of the dirt in my perennial containers come spring and fall. I work this in, paying special attention to work the compost into the soil at the natural drip line of the plant (where rain or water drips from the edge of the leaves onto the soil) to help push nutrients from the compost or fertilizer down to the roots.

I use liquid fish fertilizer every two to three weeks throughout the growing season. Fish fertilizer is a great way to give your plants nutrients with extra nitrogen, but not so much it will burn the plants.

My fish fertilizer (any gardening center carries it) is a 5–1–1 ratio, meaning it has 5 percent nitrogen, 1 percent phosphate, and 1 percent soluble potash. Most plants need more nitrogen during the growing season, especially heavy nitrogen feeders like your brassicas or cole crops (including broccoli, brussels sprouts, cabbage, cauliflower, and kale).

Go by the chart on your fertilizer bottle: for mine, it's one tablespoon per gallon of water for outdoor container plants to one cubic foot of soil.

I use an old milk carton and an old plastic measuring cup. Don't use your kitchen tablespoons; it stinks.

Pour the measured amount into your milk jug filled with water, put on cap, and shake to evenly distribute throughout the water.

It's best to water with the fertilizer when soil isn't too dry or parched, but moist. Use all the fertilizer after it's mixed. Don't store it for later uses. If you don't need the full amount, simply mix up a smaller amount.

Store the fish fertilizer out of sunlight and away from high temperatures. Try not to get it on the leaves of the plant when applying.

Stop applying the liquid fertilizer about two to three weeks before your first average frost date. You want the plant to go into its dormant state for winter, especially with perennials.

You may be wondering about making manure or compost tea. Both of these involve putting either manure or compost in a large container, filling it with water, and allowing it to "steep" until the liquid is the color of tea, and then watering your plants with the "tea." Many methods suggest you aerate and agitate the compost bucket to create an aerobic environment for the beneficial organisms to thrive. No scientific studies at this time show that applying the compost or manure tea is more beneficial than applying the manure or compost to the soil for a backyard garden, but many backyard gardeners swear by it. With manure, I'd use caution if applying on your edibles and wouldn't use anytime during the spring or harvest time.

Watering

Using the proper soil or potting mix will help, but containers will generally need to be watered more often than raised beds or in-ground gardens. The smaller the container, the more often you'll need to water. In the heat of summer, you may need to water twice a day.

Always use a watering can or gentle spray or mist when watering your containers. Direct pouring from a hose or bucket washes away soil and exposes the roots.

For larger containers, it's best to do a deep watering rather than frequent small amounts. I use a slow spray of water until water begins to come out the drain holes. I don't water again until the top two inches of soil have dried out.

However, if you let your soil get too dry, where it pulls away from the sides of the pot, water will almost immediately run out the bottom. If this happens, set the pot in a larger container of water and let it soak up water from the bottom. If the container is too large for this, apply water multiple times, preferably with a slow spray, until the soil starts to absorb moisture.

Reasons to Try Container Gardening

Pros

- less space needed
- less susceptible to pests and disease
- more control over soil and microclimate
- easier access to plants, as containers can be kept close to house
- keeps invasive plants under control
- less weeding

Cons

- container gardens and yields generally tend to be smaller than those of traditional gardens
- more investment in containers needed (rather than simply planting in the ground)
- more watering required for many types of containers
- must replenish soil with nutrients more often

IN-GROUND GARDENING

This is just as it sounds—you're growing your vegetables and fruit straight in the ground. This is how we raise most of our crops and main annual vegetable garden.

If you're putting in a new gardening spot, you'll want to kill off the existing grass and sod. You can use black plastic laid out over the ground for several months to use heat and smothering to kill off the existing plants. Another option is to use a tractor or a rototiller to break up and churn the sod, roots, and plants into easily workable soil.

This method uses the soil and dirt you already have, although you can't really go wrong adding in compost.

Reasons to Use In-Ground Gardening

Pros

- Ease. No importing of other soil or dirt, and no construction of walls or containers.

- Economy. No building materials to buy.

- Assurance. You're using existing dirt and space. You know what that piece of ground has or hasn't been treated with, which is not always the case when purchasing large quantities of top-soil for raised and container beds.

- Space control. Because you're not constricted by arm width to reach across beds, you can make your in-ground garden as large or as small as you like. This works best for large sprawling crops or corn that does best when planted in blocks for pollination.

- Water. In-ground gardens don't dry out as fast as raised beds or containers, meaning less watering for you. Because an in-ground garden is a relatively flat surface, drip irrigation, sprinklers, or soaker hoses are easy to install.

Cons

- Physical impairment. If you have any type of disability or mobility issues, in-ground gardening is harder due to bending, stooping, and kneeling.

- Compact soil. Walking between your rows of plants compacts the soil in your in-ground garden.

- Harder to amend soil based on plant. Because there's no barrier between soil areas in in-ground gardening like raised beds with walls or containers, it's harder to amend one area for a different pH level or nutrient based on one specific plant's needs.

- Drainage. If you have poor draining soil, in-ground gardening takes more compost and soil building than doing a raised bed or container with purchased soil.

- Weeds. Because there's no barrier like with containers or support walls on raised beds, existing grass or weeds will encroach on the perimeter of your in-ground garden. You can use our natural weed control strategies starting on page 113 to combat this.

There's no right or wrong garden bed type. It depends on your conditions, your space, your resources, and what works for you. As I shared, we use a measure of all three types.

GARDENING METHOD WORKSHEET

Decide which method of gardening you'll be using (it may be all three). If using containers, decide what type and size and which crops you'll be planting in your containers.

Container/crops	Raised Bed/crops	In-Ground/crops
whiskey barrel/strawberries	back slope/garlic	main summer vegetable garden

Parsley

Choosing
Your Plant
Variety
& Seeds

Choosing Your Plant Variety and Seeds

God said, "I give you every seed-bearing plant on the face of the whole earth and every tree that has fruit with seed in it. They will be yours for food."

GENESIS 1:29

You've decided what crops you're going to grow based on your family's needs, what grows best for your climate, and where you'll be planting and creating your garden.

Now it's time to decide which varieties of plants you'll be putting in. There are two options when it comes to planting: direct sow and seedlings.

Direct sow is exactly what it sounds like; take the seed and directly sow it into the soil in its permanent growing spot. We'll also discuss winter sowing, which is technically direct sowing with seed-starting aspects.

Seed starting or seedlings require you to plant the seeds in a greenhouse or indoors, usually in a small tray or pot; let the seeds sprout; and, when they're young, transplant them outdoors to their final growing spot. (We'll talk about proper seed starting later.) You can also purchase seedlings or starts from gardening centers, greenhouses, or growers in your area.

TYPES OF SEEDS

You may have heard the term *heirloom seeds* and wondered: What exactly are the differences between regular seeds and heirloom seeds? There are three types of seeds available today: heirloom seeds, hybrid seeds, and genetically modified seeds (though GMO seeds aren't found directly on regular store and garden-center shelves).

Heirloom Seeds

These seeds are open-pollinated seeds from varieties that have been handed down for generations. When planted, they will produce the same plant with the same characteristics of the parent plant you saved them from.

Heirloom seeds have much more diversity than hybrid counterparts. In my opinion (and a great many other gardeners') their produce has greater flavor depth and comes in almost all colors of the rainbow, from purple cauliflower, to red carrots, black tomatoes, and cranberry beans, just to name a few. They have history and stories, and are often named for the family or region they've been grown in for generations.

My family has been saving our own strain of pole green beans we call Tarheel beans, because my grandparents brought them with them from the hills of Appalachia when they migrated to Washington State in the early 1940s. I'm partial to a seed with history, especially one I can save and plant every year without purchasing from a store.

Hybrid Seeds

These seeds are created by companies or scientists in a lab to combine two varieties of the same plant (two types of tomatoes for example), picking the best characteristics from each variety to create a plant that is disease resistant and offers a high yield. These are available on store shelves and are not the same as GMO seeds or plants.

GMO (Genetically Modified Organism) Seeds

And finally, these seeds are created in a lab by splicing or combining different organisms (viruses, bacteria, animal DNA) to create a patented plant. For example, Monsanto created a GMO corn that has genetic material from bacteria[1], *Bacillus thuringiensis*, to produce an endotoxin. They also have GMO corn that is Roundup resistant, meaning the crops can be sprayed with the herbicide Roundup and the plant won't die, due to gene altering. Over 90 percent of domestic corn is genetically modified.[2]

The most popular GMO crops at the time of this writing are alfalfa, apples, canola, corn, cotton, papaya, soybeans, summer squash, and sugar beets.

While you won't find GMO seeds for sale on regular store shelves, in garden centers, or seed catalogs, corn will cross-pollinate across miles, which makes it harder and harder to keep strains pure without cross-contamination.

I won't get into the many debates on GMO crops and foods here, but suffice it to say my family and I have chosen to grow an all heirloom seed garden and do our best to avoid foods and crops that are known to be GMO.

Earlier blooming than Mammoth dill, this Bouquet dill has large seed umbels and dark-green foliage. Dill provides a great beneficial-insect habitat in the garden and can reseed prolifically.

Planting: Sow seeds directly after the last frost. Dill has a naturally low germination rate; 60% is typical. Can be started indoors 4-6 weeks before last frost, but doesn't like to be transplanted. Leave alone once established.

Harvesting: Harvest leaves as soon as the plant is large enough. Leave some flowers to develop into seed and harvest them when they have turned a brownish tan.

Get full planting info at www.seeds.targeteconomics.com/FFA

Which Type of Garden Seed Is Best?

The one that works best for you and your goals. You'll find I mention that quite a bit in my approach to raising your own food.

Organic seeds are from plants that were grown on certified organic land. "Organic" doesn't mean they're heirloom or hybrid, simply that the plants and seeds were grown and harvested with organic practices.

Hybrid seeds are chosen for traits that make them less susceptible to common disease, and they offer a high yield and uniformity. Think perfectly red round tomatoes instead of heirloom tomatoes with lumps and stripes but dripping with taste. Hybrid seeds must be purchased from the store every year. If you try to save seed from these plants, and if they sprout and grow for you, they will revert back to one of the parent plants, usually giving you an undesirable plant or one different than the plant you saved it from.

This happened for us with zucchini before we switched over to a full heirloom seed garden. The zucchini plant was a volunteer from one of the zucchinis I'd left in the garden the fall before. It produced a beautiful, dark-green zucchini, but every zucchini from that plant was so horribly bitter not even the livestock would eat it. You couldn't pretty it up in a cake. We pulled out the plant.

There is nothing wrong with growing hybrid seeds; please don't feel guilty if you choose to go that route. Some gardeners will plant a mix of hybrid and heirloom seeds. Some plant all heirloom seeds.

If seed saving is appealing to you, you will need to grow heirloom seeds. If you've planted all heirloom seed plants, that option is open to you. But if you decide you want to save seeds after you've planted using hybrid seeds, you'll need to wait until the following year when you've planted heirloom plants. For more information on learning to seed save, visit Familygardenplan.com to find additional resources I've created for readers of this book (which means you!).

PURCHASING YOUR SEEDS

You've come a long way already. You've decided which plants to grow based on what you eat, determined your growing season, and evaluated the land you have available. You know if you want hybrid or heirloom seeds.

There are a ton of options when it comes to ordering or buying your garden seed. When choosing each variety, you'll want to consider your growing season and the information on the seed packets.

Note: not all seed packets will contain all of this information, but they'll have most of it.

- plant name: sometimes the Latin name
- heirloom or open-pollinated if applicable

- days to germination: how many days it takes the seeds to sprout from when you place them in the dirt
- days to harvest: how many days it takes from germination until you get to begin harvesting and eating
- depth: how deep to plant the seed in the ground (general rule of thumb is the bigger the seed, the farther into the dirt it goes)
- spacing: how far apart each plant should be
- sun: whether the plant needs full sun, part sun, or shade
- when to plant: when to direct sow, when to start from seeds indoors if needed, when to put plants outside in the dirt, whether fall planting is applicable
- general care: most will give you a few sentences on any specific care that variety may need

Let your growing season determine which varieties you get. For example, if you have a short growing season like I do, you're going to look through the winter squash varieties and pick the varieties with 60 days to harvest rather than 120 days to harvest. We tend to be cooler, so I look for notes on cooler climate varieties.

If you have a longer growing season, you may want to pick two varieties so you can plant a 60-day variety for an early harvest and the 120-day variety so you have a fresh crop coming on when the first variety ends. I'll do my best not to be jealous if you can grow longer than me, because jealousy isn't becoming, right?

If you're in a hotter climate, look for varieties that indicate drought or heat resistance.

Where to Buy Seeds

Almost all grocery stores, hardware stores, and garden centers will have seed packets for sale. You may find local gardening clubs that host plant and seed exchanges in your area.

There are lots of seed catalogs you can request online, and most are free from seed companies. (There's just something about thumbing a seed catalog that makes me all kinds of happy.)

Or order and shop online. The Seed Savers Exchange is a nonprofit organization that preserves heirloom, organic, and non-GMO varieties of seeds, and you can order from their seed vault online.

HOW MUCH TO PLANT

Below you'll find a chart with average recommendations for how much to plant per person for a year's worth of food, and how much each plant produces on average. Keep in mind, these averages are based on good soil and may differ year to year. I find my tomatoes and beans produce much more than the average listed. Your actual yield will be affected by soil nutrition, weather, and pest conditions.

Bushel	Peck	Quart	Pint
4 pecks 8 gallons 32 quarts 64 pints 128 cups	8 quarts 16 pints 32 cups	2 pints 4 cups	2 cups

How Much Fruit to Plant

FRUIT	Plants per Person	Average Yield Per Plant
Apples		Dwarf: 5–6 bushels Semi-Dwarf: 10–15 bushels Standard: 5–20 bushels
Apricots		Miniature: 1–2 pecks Dwarf: 1–2 bushels Standard: 3–4 bushels
Blackberries	2–4 plants per person	35–70 cups per plant
Blueberries	2 plants per person	15–45 cups depending on maturity of plant
Cherries		**Sweet** Dwarf: 8–10 gallons Semi-Dwarf: 10–15 gallons Standard: 15–20 gallons **Sour** Dwarf: 3–5 gallons Semi-Dwarf: 12–18 gallons

FRUIT	Plants per Person	Average Yield Per Plant
Elderberries	1 plant per person	30-36 cups per mature plant
Grapes	1 vine per person	10-30 cups per vine
Nectarines		Miniature: 1–2 pecks Dwarf: 3–4 bushels Standard: 6–10 bushels
Peaches		Miniature: 1–2 pecks Dwarf: 3–4 bushels Standard: 6–10 bushels
Pears		Dwarf: 6–8 bushels Standard: 12–15 bushels
Plums		**European** Dwarf: 1–1½ bushels Standard: 1–2 bushels **Japanese** Dwarf: 3–4 bushels Semi-Dwarf: 4–5 bushels Standard: 5–6 bushels
Raspberries	10–25 plants per person	1–2 quarts per plant
Rhubarb	2–3 crowns per person	6 cups per crown
Strawberries	20–25 plants per person	1 pound or 1 pint per plant

How Many Vegetables to Plant

VEGETABLES	Average Plants per Person	Average Pounds per Plant	Average Cups per Plant
Asparagus	10–15 per person average	2–3 pounds per plant	4–6 cups
Beans, Dry	15 plants per person	¼–½ pound per plant	2 cups
Beans, Snap	Bush: 15–20 plants per person Pole: 10–15 plants per person	½ pound per plant ½ pound per plant	Bush: 2 cups Pole: 3–4 cups
Beets	36–40 per person	¼ pound per beet	½ – ¾ cup
Broccoli	3–5 plants per person	1 pound per plant	5–6 cups
Brussels Sprouts	2–3 plants per person	¾–1 pound per plant	4 cups
Cabbage (finely chopped/shredded)	3–5 plants per person	2–4 pounds per plant	8–16 cups
Carrots	25–30 per person	¼ pound per carrot	¼ cup
Cauliflower	2–3 plants per person	2 pounds per plant	3–4 cups
Celery	3–5 per person	½ pound per plant	2 cups

VEGETABLES	Average Plants per Person	Average Pounds per Plant	Average Cups per Plant
Corn (Sweet, in husk)	15 plants per person	2 ears per plant	1½ cups
Cucumbers (3–5" pickling cukes)	2–4 plants per person	3–5 pounds per plant	8–15 cups (3–5 quarts whole)
Eggplant	1–2 plants per person	8–10 pounds per plant	32–40 cups
Garlic	15 bulbs per person		
Kale	5 plants per person	1 pound per plant	3–6 cups
Leeks	12–15 plants per person	¼ pound per plant	½ cup
Lettuce	5–10 per person	¼–1 pound per plant	4–6 cups
Okra	6–8 plants per person	1 pound per plant	1½ cups
Onions, storage	15 bulbs per person	½ pound	1 cup
Parsnip	10–12 per person	⅓ pound per plant	⅔ cup

VEGETABLES	Average Plants per Person	Average Pounds per Plant	Average Cups per Plant
Peas, field	30 plants per person	⅛–¼ pound per plant	¼ cup
Peppers	Hot: 1–2 plants per person Sweet: 3–4 plants per person	1–4 pounds per plant	3–10 cups
Potatoes	10–15 plants per person	2 pounds per plant	4 cups
Pumpkins	1–2 plants per person	4–10 pounds per plant	16–40 cups cubed
Rutabagas	5–10 plants per person	1–3 pounds per plant	1½–5 cups
Spinach	15 plants per person	¼ pound per plant	1½ cups
Squash, summer (pattypan, yellow, zucchini)	1–2 plants per person	5–20 pounds per plant	12–50 cups
Squash, winter (Hubbard, banana, acorn, butternut, buttercup)	1–2 plants per person	10–15 pounds per plant	10–15 cups
Sweet Potatoes	5 plants per person	2 pounds per plant	5 cups
Tomatoes	5 plants per person	5–15 pounds per plant	7½ cups–22½ cups
Turnips	5–10 plants per person	½ pound per plant	2 cups

Look at the crops you identified on page 24 (Food Needs for a Year Worksheet) and transfer them to the worksheet that follows. On that worksheet, use the yield charts above to determine the amount you'll need to reach the desired annual yield for your family.

If you plan on preserving, especially canning, any of your garden produce, the variety can make a difference. I grow and can all our tomato products for the year; no need for store-bought tomato sauce, tomato paste, tomato soup, spaghetti sauce, pizza sauce, salsa, sun dried tomatoes, or whole tomatoes.

If this is your goal, make sure you have chosen a paste tomato for at least some of your plants. I personally love heirloom San Marzano Lungo 2 and plant a minimum of 18 of them. A paste tomato has less water, which means less simmering time, more flavor in sauces, and a thicker sauce naturally. This is a big deal come harvest and canning time.

If you plan on making cucumber pickles, plant a pickling variety. I choose the Chicago pickling cucumber. These varieties offer high yield (enough ripen at once to make a whole batch of pickles), have good flavor when pickled (not bitter), are fairly uniform in size, and are firm—no one likes a soggy pickle.

If you plan on canning salsa, make sure you plant enough jalapenos and green bell peppers to add to your tomatoes without having to purchase from the store.

Now, get the Crops for a Year Worksheet filled in and your seeds ordered!

CROPS FOR A YEAR WORKSHEET

Individual Fruits/Vegetables

Crop	Desired Annual Yield	Number of Plants Needed (use average cups per plant from the How Many Fruits/Vegetables to Plant)
green beans	39 pints (78 cups)	38 to 40 pole bean plants

Combination Recipes

Crop	Desired Annual Yield	Number of Plants Needed (use average cups per plant from the How Many Fruits/Vegetables to Plant)
tomatoes, salsa	40 cups (for 26 pints of salsa)	3 to 5 plants
onion, salsa	20 cups	20 plants
bell pepper, salsa	20 cups	4 to 6 plants
jalapeno, salsa	4 cups	1 to 2 plants
garlic, salsa	20 cloves	4 to 5 plants

Getting the Garden in the Ground

Getting the Garden in the Ground

Remember this: Whoever sows sparingly will also reap sparingly, and whoever sows generously will also reap generously.

2 CORINTHIANS 9:6

Getting all your seed packets out is akin to a fashionista getting the latest runway collection. There's something special and exciting when the air is almost pregnant with the flavor and colors of all the crops you'll soon be harvesting.

One of the biggest woes for most gardeners is the winter season (though sometimes it's a welcome rest period), when not much grows and your garden feels barren. While most gardeners won't be able to plant out much in those cold months (unless they're using season extenders), this is when you'll begin seed starting.

You can choose to purchase starts from a local greenhouse or garden center, but starting seeds at home is fairly easy and can save you quite a bit of money. It also means you get to pick and control the exact varieties you want to grow. Call me a control freak, but this plays a big part in my seed starting.

Most greenhouses and big garden centers will only have a few varieties of each plant type to pick from, usually the most popular. In my decades of gardening, I've only once seen a San Marzano Lungo heirloom tomato start for sale near me. For my heirloom-loving peeps, you'll most likely need to seed start your own to get the varieties you want. I will try not to gush at all the choices, but seriously—one must spend at least one afternoon thumbing through the tomato section of your favorite seed company.

Seed starting indoors is a great way to extend your growing season and get a harvest that much sooner. I wouldn't be able to plant tomato seeds outdoors until mid-May on a warm year, and since they take about 80 days to harvest, I'd just get tomatoes when the cold weather would set in, cutting off my harvest time. This doesn't work so well when your goal is to harvest enough tomatoes to preserve and take you through an entire year of tomato products for your family. So I seed start all my peppers and tomatoes to extend my growing season and ensure I get a large crop.

SUPPLIES FOR SEED STARTING

Here are a few items you will need to ensure success with your seed starting.

- Containers. More on this in the next section.

- Soil. We'll discuss this more in depth shortly, since soil is often overlooked and one of the biggest reasons for seedling failure.

- Light. Unless you live in a southern climate, a sunny windowsill won't provide enough light for healthy plants. I recommend a grow light. I have a four-foot grow light that fits into a corner of our living room, and I've been growing more than 20 tomato and pepper plants under it for going on five years (with the same lightbulb too).

- Heat. This is more important for heat-loving plants like peppers, but the soil temperature plays a key role in germination of all seeds, aka sprouting and growing. If you're starting seeds in your home, it will likely be warm enough for most plants, but if you're using a garage or other unheated area (or you just like to keep the house cold) you may need seed heating mats or other heat options.

Seed-Starting Containers

No matter what container you use, you'll need to make sure it's been washed and dried. If it had plants in it previously, sanitize the pots with a solution of one part bleach to ten parts water, soaking the containers for ten minutes. Wash with regular soap and water, scrub, rinse well, and allow to dry.

If you don't properly wash and sanitize your containers, you can introduce disease to your starts, which are more susceptible than older plants. We're not saving any money if our efforts die because we didn't take a simple step, right?

- **Paper egg cartons work well for starting seeds.** They're free and will biodegrade down if you decide to plant them in the ground. However, they're porous, they dry out faster, and, due to size, seedlings need to be transplanted within a few weeks. I keep mine on a rimmed metal cookie sheet to avoid any of the water leaking out and ruining the surface they're sitting on.

- **Plastic clamshells and lettuce containers.** These are some of my favorites because they create the natural greenhouse effect we need when starting seeds by simply shutting the lid. Lettuce containers with the lid are deep, so I don't need to replant many starts, especially lettuce, when using these containers. Plus, it gives new use to something I'd normally throw out. Score!

- **Milk cartons.** These have a handle for easy moving and are quite deep.

- **Newspaper pots.** Most newspapers use a soy-oil-based ink along with other additives. Though newspaper will break down, the ink (depending upon what additives are used) may not. I prefer not to put it in my garden and would remove the newspaper from the seedlings before planting. (Many gardeners do use newspaper, though. Best thing about gardening? You get to decide what works for you.) To make a newspaper pot, fold a sheet of newspaper in half longways (so you have a long skinny strip). Use a cylinder—a drinking glass, Mason jar, or tin can—and place it on the short, skinny edge of the newspaper leaving a few inches of the newspaper overhanging on the end of the container (the top ⅓ of the container will be sticking out at the top with no newspaper covering it). Roll the newspaper around the container. Turn it upside down (ends of the newspaper facing upwards) and push the loose part of the newspaper down to create a bottom. Carefully pull your rolled newspaper pot down off of your container, maintaining the cylindrical shape, and you have a little seedling pot.

- **Toilet paper or paper towel rolls.** Save these up over the year and at planting time, cut the paper towel roll into thirds (depending on how deep you want your container), then fold one end closed to hold the soil. I tried cutting a toilet paper roll in half to get two pots out of it, but found it didn't leave much room for soil and I had a harder time getting my folds to stay put. To fold, on one end bring two sides together to meet in the middle, then fold the two end points back down on top of each other. You can use a pencil to push down any ends flat from the inside if need be, before filling with soil. They'll stay upright easier if you put them in a rimmed box or container that keeps them clustered together.

- **Plastic cups.** I'm not a huge fan of buying plastic throwaway cups, but if you have some, put them to use growing your plants before recycling them.

- **One-gallon pots.** You can reuse any pots you get when purchasing plants from a nursery or garden center. You can also order new ones online or find them for sale in garden centers or departments. I keep the same pots, washing them out each year, and I use them over and over. This size pot comes in handy if you have a shorter growing season and need to let your plants grow for quite a while before putting them outside in the ground.

My tomato plants live in the one-gallon pots for close to two months after their first three weeks of life in their nursery containers. They spend close to three months inside, so they must be potted into larger one-gallon containers.

HOW TO START SEEDS SUCCESSFULLY

Use Correct Soil

Young plants are just like infants; they're more susceptible to disease and illness. If you use dirt straight out of your garden, you're introducing any disease, bacteria, or fungus that's in the soil to a baby without an immune system. This is often the cause of dampening off—a form of blight on seedlings and one of the biggest culprits of seedling death.

If you've ever started seeds indoors and suddenly they shriveled up and died, you've most likely experienced dampening off.

When using dirt out of the garden, you're also bringing insects and their eggs into the house or gardening shed. You don't want the bugs on your baby seedlings or flying and crawling about your living room, trust me.

Here are some solutions.

1. **Purchase potting soil.** I only use organic potting soil. It holds the correct ratios and has been pasteurized to kill any disease and/or fungus.

2. **Pasteurizing soil in the oven.** I'll be honest, I don't want to deal with trays and trays of dirt in my oven and haven't personally used this method. Pennsylvania State University advises to put 4 inches of moist soil (use a rimmed appropriate baking dish) in a 180 degrees Fahrenheit preheated oven, covered with foil. Insert a candy or oven thermometer into the center of the soil. When it reaches 180 degrees, bake for 30 minutes, then remove from oven and allow to cool. It's important not to let the soil reach a temperature greater than 200 degrees Fahrenheit because if soil reaches 212 degrees (we're keeping a safe buffer here) it becomes sterile and won't support plant life.[1]

3. **Make a mix of equal parts compost, top soil, and sand.** Again, you'll need to pasteurize the top soil, but this is a DIY solution.

Correct Soil Temperature

For warm-weather crops, your soil must be at least 60 degrees Fahrenheit, or warmer, for the seeds to germinate. The general rule of thumb is between 65 to 75 degrees, though your hot peppers may need to be over 80 degrees for best germination rates.

> The optimal soil temperature for best germination is the temperature at which almost 100 percent of your seeds will germinate. The cooler the soil temperature, the fewer seeds will germinate. If you get too cold, none will germinate; but I've had good success with around 65 degrees for everything except hot peppers.

You can use a soil thermometer for absolute accuracy or go by the average temperature in your home. Because the soil in your home is in a container above ground, it will be closer to the indoor temperature than outdoor conditions. In outdoor conditions, just because the air temperature is 70 degrees does not mean the soil temperature will be; but in my experience the indoor air temperature will be the soil temperature as well.

I don't use seedling mats or hot pads, the temperature in our living room is usually 65 to 75 degrees (cooler in early morning before the fire is built back up), and I haven't had an ounce of problems getting my seeds to germinate. I will place my trays of seeds about 8 inches from the fireplace while they're germinating.

Take care not to leave seedlings near a window or drafty area that will cool down at night. Once seeds are sprouted, they don't require extra heat as long as the indoor temperatures stay above 55 degrees Fahrenheit.

HOW TO START YOUR SEEDS INDOORS

Fill your prepared and chosen containers with soil. Plant your seeds according to package directions for depth. A general rule of thumb is to put the seed in the soil the same depth of the length of the seed. In other words, the smaller the seed, the shallower you plant. I place my tomato, lettuce, and pepper seeds right on the surface of the soil and thoroughly saturate the dirt. The water pushes the seed down into the soil sufficiently.

I will plant more seeds than I need in case germination rates aren't 100 percent. Don't worry; you'll thin them out later if need be. After you've placed the seeds in the dirt, water thoroughly. When germinating seeds, it's important the soil doesn't dry out. We don't want the soil to be over-saturated, just moist.

Create a greenhouse effect for germination. The best way to do this is to either cover the top of the soil with plastic wrap or use a container with a plastic lid. Vegetable seeds don't need a grow light or direct sunlight until after the seed has sprouted. I sprout all my seeds in the corner of our living room next to our woodstove, no additional light or lamps needed.

If the top of the dirt is drying out, I spray the top of the soil once a day with a spray bottle of warm water while seeds are germinating.

Once the seeds have sprouted, remove the cover and place your plants either under the grow light or in a southern-facing window. Generally, the majority of my seeds sprout at the same time; but sometimes a few will sprout later, even after removing the cover and placing them under the light. It's more important to get newly sprouted seedlings under the light and give them proper air flow by removing the covering than it is to wait for straggling seeds.

Correct Lighting

Providing your seedlings with the proper kind and amount of light is crucial to the health and growth of your seedlings after they've germinated.

Let's discuss your two options for light:

1. Sunny windowsill
2. Grow light

For most people, especially if you live in a northern climate, a sunny windowsill will not provide enough hours of daylight for your plants. You'll need six to eight hours of direct sunlight for plants a day.

If your plants are leggy, they're not receiving enough light or the light is too far away.

If you're using an artificial grow light, which is what I do, then you'll need sixteen to eighteen hours of artificial light for vegetables. I turn mine on when I get up first thing in the morning, and off when I go to bed. The light is best about four to six inches above the plants. Raise the light as the plants grow taller, keeping the distance of four inches or so above the plants.

Make sure you're using a full-spectrum lightbulb; this provides a balance of warm and cool light, mimicking the sun and nature. Many people prefer LED full spectrum because it uses less electricity.

If your plants are leggy, they're straining for more light and you need to deliver it as soon as possible to avoid weak-stemmed plants that are likely to break when put outdoors.

Create Strong Plants

Many people start seeds indoors but when they go to plant them outdoors the plants die. One possible reason is that they haven't toughened up their plants.

In nature seedlings have rain hitting them; the wind is blowing, and there is movement. This helps the stem and the roots grow deep. It develops a strong plant. It's like working out; your muscles don't grow unless they're forced to work and move against something, even if it's your own body weight for resistance.

Mimic nature

1. Place a fan on the plants periodically to mimic the wind. Make sure you only use it for short amounts of time and keep the fan on low.
2. Run your hand over the leaves and the tops of the plants. This serves the same purpose as the fan. Whenever you walk by or turn the light on or off, run your hands over the plants.
3. Use a spray bottle periodically to mimic rain. This also helps if you have low humidity in your area, and it means you don't have to water as often. Make sure your plants and the

top part of the soil dry fully between misting sessions, after the seedlings have sprouted (germinated) and have their first sets of leaves.

Note of caution when using a spray bottle to water: In outdoor settings, we don't want to use overhead watering on tomatoes (or other plants susceptible to blight, a fungal disease), but I've never had an issue when using this method indoors with seedlings. It's important your seedlings have adequate air flow and you let the top of the soil dry out before watering again. I only use the spray bottle periodically, mainly when the seedlings are small and I don't want the stream of water from a larger container washing away the dirt from the still tiny root system before they've been repotted into large containers.

Let's talk mold and fungal growth. It is very common to see a white, mold-looking substance on the surface of the soil, especially for seedlings that spend weeks inside. This is usually a sign of high humidity and too much moisture. It's not actually mold, but a fungus.

To combat it, don't water as often, let the top of the soil dry out more than you have been, and give the plants more air flow. I've found some of my plants will begin to grow fungus toward the end of their time indoors. As soon as I begin the hardening-off period ("hardening off" means gradually conditioning your seedlings to outdoor conditions), when I set the pots outside for short periods to acclimate the plants to their new environment, the fungus will be gone by the next day.

Alternatively, you can use the fan on low for an hour or so.

When to Thin Seedlings and Move to Larger Containers

What's the point of thinning out all these seeds you worked so hard to get growing? And while we're at it, why not just plant them all in big containers to begin with and skip this extra step?

It can be hard to thin out your seedlings, or any garden crop (I'm talking to you, beets and carrots), but it's necessary if you are to give each plant the space it needs to grow. If you don't thin them, you'll hamper the growth of all the plants. With seedlings, there's simply not enough soil or room in containers to sustain them all, both in nutrients and root development. So you must thin.

We don't plant in large containers to begin with because it's much harder to regulate temperatures, humidity, and soil warmth with large pots of soil. Also, it can be hard to keep those tiny seeds evenly spaced. I watch out for when my seedlings have developed their first set of true leaves (not the very first leaves you see when they sprout—their true leaves are actually the second set and will have the shape of that plant; think more saw-toothed if a tomato, frilly fingers for carrots, and ruffled curls for curly kale). Then I transplant them to larger containers to continue growing indoors under their grow light.

At this time, I can separate out each plant from their sprouting cells (I often have two or even three tomato seeds per egg carton hole) and I plant each plant in its own pot rather than thinning and tossing them. If a few don't make it through the transplanting process (normally I don't lose many, but occasionally one or two don't make it out of the 20 or so I plant), I still have a buffer. I'd rather have too many plants than not enough. I can give some away or decide to cull them when it's time to plant outdoors.

When transplanting your new little sprouts, take care not to damage their roots. Make a well inside a new, larger pot of dirt, making sure it's deep enough for you to set the roots in it, and then backfill with extra soil. It should be deep enough that the soil line hits the seedling on the same place of the stem it did in their smaller pot. Tomatoes are an exception; bury them deeper because they'll sprout new roots from the stem and create a stronger plant.

Gently tamp the soil down around the plant to help anchor it until the roots can extend and do their job. Always water plants when transplanting and add in more dirt if needed. Sometimes water will wash the dirt down into air pockets and cause it to settle, possibly leaving the top roots exposed.

Correct Hardening Off

This is where I see many people make the biggest mistake with their seedlings. They don't harden them off properly or for long enough.

If you take your plants from the protected and controlled environment of indoors or the greenhouse and plop them outdoors, you're going to put them into shock and most likely kill all of them. You must slowly introduce the plants to the outdoors, for short periods of time. Here's how I do it.

Pick a sheltered spot outdoors. Start somewhere out of direct, hot sunlight that isn't out in the open where they'll be whipped by the wind and elements. If it's 85 degrees Fahrenheit outside and your plants are used to being indoors in partial sun at 70 degrees, they're going to be stressed by the shock, even for only two hours the first day.

If it is really hot out when you start, find a spot in the shade for the first few days. Begin at least one week in advance before planting outdoors.

Seedling Hardening-Off Schedule

- Start in a protected area 2 hours the first day

- Increase by 1 to 2 hours each day over 7 to 10 days

- Gradually move them to their final planting spot (by day 5 of the hardening-off schedule, I'll place the plants where I'll be planting them, which is in direct sunlight and without any wind protection)

It can be hard to increase the hours per day your seedlings spend outdoors when you're working away from home. I start my plants on a Friday afternoon or evening, increasing the schedule according to the times above over Saturday and Sunday. By Monday I can leave them outdoors for almost eight hours. When I worked away from home, I set them out right before I left for work, and my husband (who got home before I did) brought them in when he first arrived home.

Consequently, if the weather changes drastically (we've had a few years when a cold spell came in unexpectedly), I bring the tomatoes back in the house and start the process over again once the conditions change back to the positive. It's better to have more days of hardening off before setting them out and planting them than it is to hurry up the process.

By slowly hardening off your seedlings, you'll help them gain strength and resistance—without shocking them.

How to Transplant Seedlings Successfully Outdoors

You've done it! You've grown your plants from a seed, nurtured them indoors, hardened them off, and are ready to put them in their final growing spot. From chapter 1, you've already determined it's the right time to plant and picked the best locations for your garden based on your property, gardening zone, and microclimates.

Now it's time to plant. Picking the correct spot now will save a lot of trouble later. Remember, with your hard work and the help of the information within these pages, your seedlings are going to grow and become large, productive plants.

Just as we looked at trees and different landscape items blocking light or causing adverse reactions to our plants, we now need to think about what other garden plants will be going in around our seedlings. My pole beans grow to over six feet tall if provided enough support. Certain varieties of corn will reach heights upwards of ten feet, and sunflowers are known to tower. This means if

you plant them in front of your peppers and summer squash, as the season continues, they can block the sun from anything directly behind them.

While this is advantageous for cool-weather crops in the height of summer heat—like kale, lettuce, spinach, and brassicas—it's not desirable for heat-loving plants like tomatoes and peppers.

Take care to plan out the best spot for your transplants in relation to your entire garden before nestling them into the ground in their final growing space.

To plant, dig a hole a little bit wider and deeper than the container your seedling is in. When the hole is dug, set the pot down into it to measure if it's deep enough or too deep (if you're using an egg carton or other multi-cell container, eyeball it to your best ability). We want the soil to be at approximately the same spot above the root crown as it is in the pot, or just slightly above it.

Take the end of your spade and break up the dirt at the bottom of the hole if it's compacted. If your seedling is not root-bound (you don't see the roots circling the bottom of the pot, sticking out the bottom drain holes, or in a tight web of white up the sides), gently remove the seedling with as much dirt as possible and set it inside the planting hole. Our goal is to disturb the roots as little as possible.

If your plant is root-bound, you'll know it when you remove it from the container; the roots will likely keep the dirt in the same shape as the pot, even when free. If the roots are small, you can use your fingers to tear them loose; if larger, use a gardening knife or the side of your spade to cut them free. I will make four cuts—think north, east, south, west—along the side of the roots and spread them out. It's also a good idea to make note that next year you need to either put them in larger pots or plant them sooner, if possible, to avoid them becoming root-bound.

You don't want to leave them in the root-bound shape, or the roots will continue to grow this way, never spreading out and down to establish a good root system or reaching new soil to provide better nourishment to the plant. To avoid this, I make a small cone of soil in the bottom of the hole and spread the roots out and down around it. This helps support the plant and the roots' optimal growth pattern.

Backfill soil into the hole, covering the roots, until the hole is completely filled. Firm down the dirt around the base of the plant to help fill in any air pockets and keep the plant upright until its roots are established. This is a gentle press, not a deep compression of the dirt.

Give your newly planted starts a good drink of water. It's best to use a watering can or something producing small, individual streams of water. If you use a large bucket or splash of water, you may wash away the soil and expose the roots.

I prefer to amend with any needed fertilizer to the entire bed or garden area (a single row versus a single hole) before planting and occasionally provide a top dressing if needed. For further information on amending your soil, see chapter 9.

The slight exception to this is with my tomatoes.

Planting Tomatoes

Tomatoes are somewhat fussy plants compared to others in the garden, especially if you live in a cool or wet climate. But with these troubleshooting tips, I've turned my tomato woes into a tomato harvest that takes us through an entire year of not having to buy tomato and spaghetti sauce, salsa, or stewed tomatoes from the store.

1. Never plant tomatoes in the same spot of soil you had tomatoes, peppers, or potatoes in the year before.

2. Plant tomatoes deep—all the way up to their first set of leaves—to encourage a large root system for a healthier plant.

3. Add some compost to the bottom of the hole when you plant, if needed.

4. Tomatoes like a soil pH of 6.5 to 7.2 and need calcium to combat blossom-end rot. If your soil shows low calcium levels (a soil test is best to determine your levels—see chapter 9), you can add lime or crushed-up egg shells to help bring acidic soil (lower numbers on the pH scale) up and add calcium to the soil. Place up to three-quarters of a cup of gardening lime on the bottom of the hole or one to two crushed-up eggshells, and work into the soil. Gardening lime will increase alkalinity of soil so only use if you know your current pH level and doing so won't change soil from optimal pH range.

   Note: if you don't have slightly acidic soil to begin with, egg shells may not break down enough to provide extra calcium to your tomatoes. If using egg shells, it's best to powder them in a coffee or spice grinder or, alternatively, soak them in vinegar, let dry, and crush up before putting them in soil. You can also do a top dressing by working crushed-up eggshells or gardening lime into the soil around the drip line of the plant.

5. If using cages or support systems that go into the ground around the plant, put them in upon planting so you don't pierce the root system when the plant is bigger.

6. Make sure tomatoes are planted in full sun; they don't do well in shady or damp areas.

DIRECT SOWING

Direct sowing seed is pretty, well, direct. You're taking the seed and putting it directly into the soil. However, you can follow a few basic tips to improve your germination rate (how long from when you put the seed in the dirt to when it sprouts).

You'll want to follow the Seed Starting and Planting Chart on page 97 and make sure your soil temperature is warm enough for direct sowing. We watch the forecast and prefer to plant when it's sunny (or cloudy but dry) with rain due the next day.

When I was growing up, my father always soaked his bean seed before planting. We've additionally found it helpful to soak several types of seed for faster sprouting. It tends to work best with larger seeds such as peas, beans, corn, and beets.

How to Soak Seeds

Place seeds in a shallow container or small bowl. Fill with cool, fresh water (we're on a private well, so chlorine isn't an issue) until seeds are covered.

Soak larger seeds overnight or for approximately eight hours in room-temperature water before planting. We soak beans, peas, corn, and beet seeds (beets especially perform better when soaked). Some sources say not to let beet seed soak in water overnight but instead to place them on a damp towel. We haven't experienced any issues with germination, but you may want to test it yourself. I don't generally bother soaking the smaller seeds like lettuce or carrots. Drain seeds right before planting.

Your seed packets should have instructions for planting depth, but again, as a general rule of thumb, however large the seed, that's how deep you plant it. Small seeds like carrot, dill, and lettuce only need a light covering of soil.

Either poke a hole in the ground to the appropriate depth (first knuckle works great for things like squash and bean seed) or dig a shallow trench the correct planting depth and drop the seeds in. After placing the seed in the dirt, cover back with soil and water.

It's very important that your seeds not dry out during the germination period; they need to stay moist. You don't want to drown them, but moisture is key in getting them to sprout.

Seed-Sowing Depth

- small seeds, like carrot, dill and lettuce: ⅛ to ¼ inch deep

- beets, parsnips, and turnips: ¼ to ½ inch deep

- beans, cucumber, peas, and squash: approximately 1 inch deep

- corn: 1½ to 2 inches deep

WINTER SOWING

Winter sowing seeds is an excellent way to get a jump-start on the growing season without the aid of grow lights, heat, or hardening off.

For winter sowing, begin by creating little mini greenhouses with plastic containers to grow your vegetables outdoors. You set the seeds out in the middle of winter or late spring (some people do it when there's still a lot of snow on the ground) inside their little greenhouses and let nature do its thing.

Common containers are used milk jugs, plastic clam shells from apples, or plastic lettuce containers with the hinged lids. Make sure the container is at least three inches deep.

If using a milk jug or container that doesn't have a lid, take the scissors about two-thirds or three-quarters of the way up from the bottom and cut approximately two-thirds of the way around, leaving a hinge portion around the handle so you can place soil and seeds inside and still seal the container back up.

Containers need both drain holes on the bottom and air holes on the top for ventilation. Make sure the holes on top are large enough for rain water to get inside and provide moisture for the seeds and plants.

For a milk jug, I use a pair of scissors and stab four decent-sized holes in the bottom of the jug. Leave the lid off and stab about three to four more holes along the top for extra ventilation and water access.

I tried it last year with tomatoes, peppers, lettuce, kale, and cabbage. While the tomatoes and peppers did sprout, it wasn't until mid-June, which is much too late for my area to expect any type of harvest. If you have a longer growing season, you can try this method with warm-weather plants, but I am only doing it for cool-weather crops.

Note: Whenever trying something new, if it's a crop you depend upon like we do with our tomatoes, always make sure you use a tried-and-true method with the majority of your crop during the first test.

How to Plant Your Seeds

Once you have your containers prepared, fill them up with approximately three inches of potting soil. It's still important to use sterile soil to help keep any pathogens or disease away from the young seedlings.

Spray water over the soil both to get it wet and test your drain holes. Make sure they're big enough for the water to get out.

Sow your seeds. After seeds are sown, seal up your container. If using a hinged lettuce container or clam shell, simply snap it closed. For your milk jugs, use a couple of strips of duct tape to secure the openings.

Use a permanent marker on the container to record the seed type you have planted. You may choose to mix a few seeds in the same container or have each container dedicated to one type of plant. Up to you!

Set the container in your garden area, or somewhere it won't be disturbed but will receive natural rainfall for the next weeks or months.

Care of Seedlings Once Sprouted

Once seeds have sprouted, open the lid during warm, sunny days, but close it at night until outdoor temps are warm enough for the specific plant. The beauty of winter sowing is you don't have to harden it off; simply plant it right into the soil.

Seeds will naturally sprout when conditions are right. Most cool-weather seeds will sprout about three weeks before the last average frost date, though you can set the winter-sown seeds out any time of year.

Transplant out of the little greenhouses following the outside planting dates found on the seed packet or in your Seed Starting and Planting Chart on the next page.

Seed starting can be a great advantage to your garden, allowing you a much longer harvest time. In some climates, it's the only way you'll successfully be able to grow a crop. It's the only way I can grow enough tomatoes and peppers to take us through a whole year.

Below is the seed starting and planting chart I use. You won't find all vegetables listed because some plants don't do well started indoors or don't warrant the work for only a few days earlier harvest.

SEED STARTING AND PLANTING CHART

Plant	Start Indoors	Germination Period	Direct Sow (spring and fall dates if applicable for fall crops)	My Sow Date My last frost date_____ My first frost date _____
Basil	4–8 weeks, plant outside 2–3 weeks after last frost	5–10 days	2–4 weeks after last frost	
Beans— bush, pole, and shelled	You can start indoors on the last frost date, but beans don't like their roots messed with, and I prefer to direct sow	6–18 days	3–4 weeks after last frost	
Beets	3 weeks before last frost, plant outside on last frost date	5–21 days	2–4 weeks before last frost and sow up to 8 weeks before first frost in fall	
Broccoli	7 weeks before last frost, plant outside 2 weeks before last frost	4–20 days	2 weeks before last frost, 10–12 weeks before first frost in fall	
Brussels sprouts	2–3 weeks before last frost, plant outside 2 weeks after last frost	5–15 days	2 weeks after last frost, can direct sow 10 weeks before first frost in fall	
Cabbage	6 weeks before last frost, plant outside 2 weeks before last frost	4–20 days	2 weeks before last frost, 6 to 8 weeks before first frost in fall	
Carrots		7–21 days	2–4 weeks before last frost, 8 to 12 weeks before first frost in fall	
Cauliflower	8–10 weeks before last frost, plant outside 4 weeks before last frost. Fall crop start 12–14 weeks before first frost, plant outside 8 weeks before first fall frost	4–10 days	2 weeks before last frost	
Chard	4 weeks before last frost, plant outside last frost date	5–21 days	Last frost date, 10–12 weeks before first frost date in fall	
Cilantro/ Coriander	4–8 weeks before last frost, plant outside right at last frost	5–10 days	2 weeks before last frost, 6–8 weeks before first frost in fall	
Corn	Best direct sown	3–10 days	2 weeks after last frost	

Plant	Start Indoors	Germination Period	Direct Sow (spring and fall dates if applicable for fall crops)	My Sow Date My last frost date_____ My first frost date _____
Cucumber (see Summer Squash)				
Dill	Best direct sown	2–3 weeks	4 weeks after last frost or when soil temp is 60 degrees Fahrenheit or warmer	
Garlic			Plant cloves in ground between 2 weeks before and 2 weeks after first frost in fall for summer harvest. Mild winter climates can plant bulbs 8–10 weeks before last frost in spring for late summer harvest if ground isn't frozen	
Kale	3–6 weeks before last frost, plant outdoors 2–3 weeks before last frost	4–9 days	2–4 weeks before last frost, 6–8 weeks before first frost in fall	
Lettuce	6–8 weeks before last frost, plant outdoors 3 to 4 weeks before last frost	2–15 days	2–4 weeks before last frost and 6–8 weeks before first frost in fall	
Marjoram	2–3 weeks; plant outside after all danger of frost has passed	8–10 weeks	1 week after last frost	
Melon	Last frost date, plant outdoors 4 weeks after last frost	4–10 days	4 weeks after last frost	
Okra	6–4 weeks before last frost, plant outside 4 weeks after last frost	5–12 days	4 weeks after last frost	
Onion	10–16 weeks before last frost	7–28 days	bulbs 6 weeks before or 4 weeks after last frost	
Parsnip		10–21 days	2 weeks before last frost through 12 weeks before first frost in fall	
Pea	8 weeks before last frost, plant outside 4 weeks before last frost	6–17 days	4–6 weeks before last frost through 12 weeks before first frost in fall	
Pepper	4–8 weeks before last frost (in cooler climates I recommend 8 weeks)	Hot, 14–28 days Sweet, 7–14 days	Put seedlings out 3–4 weeks after last frost	
Potato			2–4 weeks before last frost in spring	
Radish		3–10 days	2–4 weeks before last frost in spring through 8 weeks before first frost in fall	

Plant	Start Indoors	Germination Period	Direct Sow (spring and fall dates if applicable for fall crops)	My Sow Date My last frost date_____ My first frost date_____
Spinach	8–6 weeks before last frost, plant out 4 weeks before last frost	5–21 days	6 weeks before last frost in spring through 6 weeks before first frost in fall	
Squash, Summer and Winter	2 weeks before last frost	3–10 days	2–4 weeks after last frost	
Summer Savory	6–8 weeks; plant outdoors after all danger of frost has passed	2–3 weeks	1 week after last frost	
Sweet Potato			3–4 weeks after last frost in spring	
Tomato	2–8 weeks before last frost (8–10 weeks for cold climates)	5–14 days		
Turnip		5–10 days	2–4 weeks before last frost, 4 weeks before first frost in fall	

Seed Starting Checklist

Now that you've established the crops you'll be seed starting, here's an easy checklist and worksheet to help make sure you have all the supplies you'll need to get those darlings started!

Checklist of Supply Options		Action Plan	Notes
Soil	❏ purchase potting soil ❏ homemade potting soil	Purchase/ready by date: Where I'm purchasing soil or ingredients to make my own:	
Containers for seed starting	❏ egg cartons ❏ clam shell/lettuce ❏ peat pots ❏ homemade toilet or paper towel tubes ❏ plastic cups ❏ store-bought pots	How many containers do I need based on the Crops for a Year chart on page 70:	
Lighting	❏ southern exposure or sunny windowsill ❏ grow light ❏ homemade grow light with full-spectrum lightbulb	Purchase/ready by date: Where I'm purchasing my supplies/light: Location of light/seeds:	

Caring for Your Garden

Caring for Your Garden

*It is a land the L*ORD *your God cares for; the eyes of the L*ORD *your God are continually on it from the beginning of the year to its end.*

DEUTERONOMY 11:12

You've done it. The garden is in and growing. Soon you'll be harvesting lovely little darlings. This is the gardener's lull time, when the plants are in the ground and we're waiting for the production to begin.

It's also the time when you may notice pests are eating the leaves of your plants, leaves are wilting, or powdery mildew has covered your squash leaves. While I'd love to tell you that disease and pests rarely bother a well-loved garden, it wouldn't be true.

Good news: we can do many things to prevent and treat our plants naturally when maladies befall them. Rest assured, no matter how good a gardener you may be, at one time or another, you will be faced with some type of trouble in the garden.

Later, we will cover some advanced topics like addressing our soil pH, nutrient levels, crop rotation, and companion planting. The healthier a plant is (which all starts in the soil) the better chance it has of not falling to disease or recovering if hit with something.

First, we'll look at some common pests and diseases, along with ways to prevent and treat them. For readers in the United States, I highly recommend becoming familiar with your local county extension agriculture office, since some pests and diseases are very regional. Their services are free and a wealth of information. Most have organic options listed as well.

HOW TO PREVENT COMMON PESTS AND DISEASES

Your number one defense is to be in your garden daily. If an infestation or disease begins, early detection is key.

Manual removal of bugs and pests is often the best and most effective control. Flea beetles, aphids, horn worms, and squash bugs can all be removed manually.

Inspect your plants, especially if you see wilting or holes in the leaves. Make sure you inspect on the underside of the leaf for eggs or clusters of small bugs and immediately remove them. Wear a pair of gloves if touching them gives you the heebie-jeebies and dispose of eggs and bugs in a container of water, a tightly enclosed container, or by burning them.

Aphids can be knocked off with a strong spray of water, but you'll want to check every day and make sure they're not spreading to other plants in the garden.

Inspect every morning and evening, removing any sign of eggs or bugs. Depending upon the insect and their egg cycle, this may take a few weeks.

Natural Spray Options

Another organic option is to use neem oil (it's kind of like the Swiss army knife against garden pests and diseases). Neem oil is from the African neem tree. Specifically it contains the chemical compound *azadirachtin*, which is what we're after for insect control. It works as an antifeedant (they don't want to eat it), repellent, and repugnant agent and induces sterility in soft-bodied insects, mites, sap-sucking and plant-eating insects.[1] Make sure you check the ingredient label for 100 percent cold pressed neem oil; some sprays say neem oil on the label to seem natural, but contain other synthetic ingredients.

Not only is neem oil a natural pesticide and miticide, but it's also a natural fungicide. Neem oil can be used to treat powdery mildew, black spot, downy mildew, anthracnose (a group of fungal diseases), rust, leaf spot, botrytis (fungal disease), needle rust, scab and flower, twig and tip blight, early blight, and alternaria (a fungus). That's a mouthful! But the beauty is, neem oil is a multi-purpose treatment. For a detailed chart with disease description and management control visit https://plantpathology.ca.uky.edu/files/mg_ch6_appendix.pdf.

It's best to spray your plants with neem oil in the early morning or late evening on a dry day without a lot of wind; you don't want to apply it in the heat of the day or in temperatures above 80 degrees Fahrenheit. Follow the instructions for dilution on your bottle and make sure to thoroughly soak the leaves, including the undersides. Wear long sleeves, pants, and protective clothing; even though its natural, it's best to take precautions.

General application recommendations for an acute infestation or onset of disease are every 7 days. Once symptoms are gone, apply every 14 days. For preventative measures, every 14 days is recommended.

Want a homemade option? My friend Jill Winger from ThePrairieHomestead.com has a homemade DIY vegetable spray recipe she allowed me to share with you. The ingredients work together to create a repellent spray for insects.

Organic Pest Control Garden Spray Recipe

Makes one gallon

1 medium onion

4 cloves garlic

2 cups mint leaves or 20 drops peppermint essential oil

2 tablespoons cayenne pepper

2 tablespoons liquid castile soap

   (regular dish soap is actually a detergent and not desirable to use on your plants)

water

1. Place onion, garlic, peppermint, and cayenne in a blender or food processor and pulverize them.

2. Allow mixture to soak/steep for a couple of hours if possible, and then strain with a fine mesh strainer.

3. Add the onion/garlic mixture to a one-gallon container (old milk or vinegar jugs will work). Add soap and enough water to make one gallon.

4. Pour into a spray bottle and spritz on any plants being attacked by bugs.

5. Spray 1–2 times per week, or after a heavy rain.

Notes: Apply in the evening and don't spray directly on the fruit or part of the plant you'll be harvesting from soon unless you want your tomato and lettuce to taste like mint, garlic, onion, cayenne, and a wee bit of soap.

Another common garden disease is mildew. Mildew is a fungus; the two most common types are powdery and downy mildew. Powdery mildew is characterized by round, white spots anywhere on the leaf's surface and yellowing after a while. It often looks like a dusting of flour on your leaves. Powdery mildew usually shows up when you have cool nights with dry weather and high humidity. (We usually get some of this every summer on our squash plants).

Downy mildew is characterized by fungus spots that are angular and gray in appearance with fuzz on the bottom of leaves. The leaves might turn yellow before you see the spots, and fungus is limited by the veins of the leaf, meaning you'll clearly see each vein on the leaf between the yellowing, creating strips of yellow.

Though both are different fungi, the treatment is similar. Prevention-wise, make sure your plant has adequate space for air flow (vertical planting helps with this) and avoid watering at night where prolonged wet conditions favor fungal growth. If any leaves have died or turned yellow, remove them and *don't* put them in your compost pile.

The good news is, in a vegetable garden powdery mildew rarely kills a plant (though it can stunt your harvest), and there are several treatment options. Neem oil is an effective treatment for mildew, but we've got a few more.

Two old-fashioned methods involve common ingredients in your kitchen. Researchers at Cornell University discovered effective fungicidal properties of one tablespoon baking soda plus 2½ tablespoons of horticulture oil in 1 gallon of water for powdery mildew treatment on roses with experimental use.[2]

Another old-time treatment is to use milk or whey. In a study by Australian Plant Pathology, milk and whey were tested on powdery-mildew–infected grapevines, and it started working within 24 hours.[3]

With any type of spray treatment, it's best to use in the early morning or late evening and to fully saturate both sides of the leaves. It's also a good idea to do a small test area on one plant to see how it behaves before spraying your entire crop.

Another organic pest control method we use is *food grade* diatomaceous earth, or DE. DE is a white powder made from crushed-up, fossilized remains of phytoplankton. When sprinkled on exoskeletons like those of ants, fleas, and mites, it compromises the coating of their skeleton (like tiny shards of glass) and kills them. It doesn't cut your skin but it does tend to dry it out, so you may wish to use gloves.

Diatomaceous earth is a very fine powder. Take care you don't breathe it in, and don't apply on a windy day. The one drawback is that any moisture (even heavy morning dew) makes it ineffective. It's best to apply it on a dry day in the morning *after* the dew has dried. Sprinkle it on the leaves of your plants that are being chewed by insect critters, careful to *not get it on any blossoms* (we need to protect our honey bees). A mason jar with holes poked in the top of a lid to create a shaker works well. Reapply after rain or dew as needed.

Ants can be a nuisance, but unless you have an excessive amount or fire ants, I wouldn't worry about seeing them in the garden. If you see a large number, it can be a sign you have an aphid problem. Ants eat the secretions left behind by aphids and will help protect aphids because they're a food source for them. Smart critters, aren't they?

In this case, take care of the aphids and the ants. The most effective way I've found for dealing with ants is to mix up a paste of borax, sugar, and just enough water to create the paste. Place on a small saucer (make sure ants can easily crawl to the powder) and put it near their nest or where you see the ants. (Using a saucer means the paste is not in contact with my soil or plants.) They'll carry it back to the nest and it will kill the colony. It can take a week, and I recommend doing this several times to make sure you get the full nest. Make sure dogs and cats can't access the borax mixture (a wire cage secured down over the dish is a good option) and if it rains, put out a new mixture.

If you find your brassica crops being eaten by dreaded little worms, you most likely have cabbage loopers (these are my nemesis), cabbage moths, and/or diamondback moths laying eggs in your plants. The presence of small, white butterflies during the day or grayish moths in the evening (diamondbacks have a diamond pattern) means you'll likely soon find little worms eating up your plants.

Crop and row-cover cloth are organic, no-spray methods for getting rid of these worms on cabbage and cauliflower. Manually remove and dispose of any worms you see and place garden cloth or a row cover over plants in the early part of the season (spring and summer) when moths are laying their eggs. We have fewer of these pests in our fall crops.

Neem oil is also effective against cabbage moths, but you'll need to be diligent about applying every 7 to 14 days during the late spring and summer.

Another pest control measure is *Bacillus thuringiensis* (Bt). You'll often see Bt listed as a form of organic pest control (it's a strain of soil-borne bacteria) but due to the way it works in the intestines there is concern that commercial Bt, especially in genetically modified crops, combined with other herbicide sprays over long-term use may have a negative impact on human immune and hormonal systems. An investigation of the impact on the intestinal microbiome after consumption shows it may be harmful.[4] I realize most of us aren't growing genetically modified crops with other herbicide use, but I still think it's important to look at the research.

We haven't personally used Bt in our garden. I encourage you to do your own research to decide if it's an item you wish to have in your pest-fighting arsenal. Bt is listed as an approved organic method of pest control.

When it comes to vine borers, I don't have personal experience. Don't throw this book across the room if you're struggling with them, but living in the Pacific Northwest, thankfully, this isn't a pest we deal with.

But there are varying options for dealing with this devastating little moth and larvae. The most effective is to use row covers or netting to prevent the moth from laying her eggs in the first place, though you will need to hand pollinate blossoms as it blocks all insects. Diligent removal of eggs, using a trap crop like Blue Hubbard, and rotating squash planting areas are all helpful treatment methods.

According to Abby Seaman of the New York State Integrated Pest Management Program at Cornell University, neem oil, thyme oil, and kaolin clay are organic options labeled for use against the squash vine borer.[5]

Speaking of pests, let's talk about the larger creatures in the room… er garden. Deer, elk, squirrels, rabbits, groundhogs (aka woodchucks), slugs, and birds are the biggest pests to our fruit trees and garden.

In our experience, the barrier method is the most effective. We fence off our garden and put netting around the fruit trees and blueberry bushes. Deer don't bother our blueberry bushes, but the birds will strip an entire row of blueberries within a day or two when not covered.

Other methods below are shared from readers in my Homesteading Facebook group.

- "We wrap the bottom foot of our garden in hardware cloth that is buried 12 inches deep and then 6-8 inches out; so when they dig at the fence or further out they hit the hardware cloth. Hubby does nuisance wildlife removal/prevention for a living." *Debbie T.*

- "I put hardware cloth around all my fruit trees and bushes to keep rabbits out. To keep squirrels from digging up my flower garden bulbs, I encase the bulbs in chicken wire and then plant them. I have both rabbits and squirrels but the rabbits do a lot more damage than squirrels do! I have cats and they do go after them, but it can be pretty hit and miss." *Virginia R.*

- "We have a golden retriever, and of course she sheds a good bit. I gather up her hair and spread it about outside. Seems to help with the squirrels and rabbits, maybe not so much with the groundhogs!!" *Edye W.*

- "Cats and my menfolk. The cats hunt, and the menfolk 'mark their territory.' Adolescent male urine seems to be particularly effective!!" *Leah R.*

- "I used Irish Spring soap this year and didn't lose one item to the critters. I live in the country and we have all the above plus deer. Last year they ate the beans and sweet potatoes. I cut it in small pieces and wrapped it in cheesecloth. Then hung that from shepherd hooks all around the garden. I sprinkled shavings around the ground for the smaller critters." *Darlene D.*

- "I planted sunflowers for the first time this year on the opposite side of my yard from where my garden is located. The squirrels didn't even notice my tomatoes until all the sunflower seeds were eaten. By that time the tomatoes were almost done." *Jennifer I.*

Dogs and cats were listed as the best deterrent to both large and smaller pests. If using a repellent method such as human hair, urine, or soap, you'll likely need to reapply frequently throughout the gardening season. Some people swear by hot pepper, pepper plants, and essential oils; and others say they didn't work for them. Your garden truly is an experiment for you.

We've tried human hair, fake owls, shiny ribbons and CDs to repel animals, but none worked long term. The human hair needs to be replaced due to scent loss.

Slugs love damp and warm areas, like Pacific Northwest summers. They come out primarily at night or on rainy days, and their telltale signs of slime and chew marks let you know you've had a visitation.

They hide during hot weather, so keeping mulch and debris away from the base of your plants

(especially those getting hit hard) is key. Lift up any board, rock, or planter, and you'll often find slugs hanging out; and if I go barefoot, it's one of the few things that makes me cringe when I step on one. Dispose of them in soapy water or squash them—your choice. Don't use salt; it can build up and harm your soil.

Beer traps are popular; they're just shallow dishes filled with beer set around the garden that attract and then drown the slugs. Check daily to dispose of slugs and fill with new beer (they're attracted to the malt). Copper tape set around the base of plants is also recommended, though we've never tried it and reports vary on effectiveness.

I've tried egg shells (sharp edges to deter them) but haven't found it to be effective here.

Remember that proper soil care, crop rotation, adequate space for air flow, and using companion planting will all naturally help with your garden pests and diseases; but should excess pests or disease strike, you have several options to help you keep them under control.

Organic Pest and Disease Chart

Pest	Organic Method	
Insects		
ants	• food grade diatomaceous earth	• borax and sugar paste
aphids	• strong spray of water/manual removal • organic homemade pest spray	• food grade diatomaceous earth
flea beetles, horn worms, spider mites, and squash bugs	• manual removal • organic homemade pest spray	• food grade diatomaceous earth
cabbage loopers, cabbage moths, and diamondback moths	• row cloths/covers • neem oil • manual removal of worm/larvae	• Organic Homemade Pest Spray • *Bacillus thuringiensis* Bt
slugs	• manual removal	• beer trap
vine borers	• row cloths/covers • neem oil • manual removal of worm/larvae • organic homemade pest spray	• thyme oil • kaolin clay • trap crop: Blue Hubbard squash
Small and Large Animals		
birds	• netting • reflective tape/CDs	• fake owls • cat or dog

Pest	Organic Method	
deer	• guard dog • human hair • fencing	• netting • soap: Irish Spring • urine
rabbits	• hardware cloth • cat or dog	• soap: Irish Spring • chicken wire
squirrels	• cat or dog • chicken wire • hardware cloth	• soap: Irish Spring • trap crop: sunflowers
Disease		
alternaria, anthracnose, black spot, botrytis, early blight, leaf spot, needle rust, rust, scab and flower, twig and tip blight	• neem oil	
downy mildew, powdery mildew	• neem oil • baking soda and water spray • milk or whey	

NATURAL WEED CONTROL

We must talk about the elephant in the garden: weeds. I must confess, weeding isn't high on my list of fun gardening tasks. I love the way the garden looks after weeding, but the actual act, not my fave. But good weed control is important for a large harvest, especially with crops that don't produce well if competing for nutrients with said weeds (onions and asparagus, I'm talking to you).

If weeding brings up visions of hours bent over or on hands and knees pulling weeds, take heart; this doesn't have to be the case, my friends. Like most things in the garden, there are several options, and I'll leave it to you find the one that works the best for your situation. Rest assured, all of them are natural.

Natural Weed Control Methods

Like most gardeners, you'll find what works best for you, and it will probably involve several different methods. These have been effective for us without using harmful herbicides that stay in the soil for years and are a known human carcinogenic.

1. **Mulch.** Usually either hay/straw, wood chips, or sawdust. All the options work by starving the weeds of sunlight provided it's deep enough. The use of wood chips was made popular by Paul Gautschi, founder of Back to Eden Gardening, and author/gardener Ruth Stout brought the use of hay as weed control to the masses. The key to mulching is spreading

the hay and wood chips on the top of the soil thickly enough to block the light for weed control. The beauty of these methods is that they not only help block weeds but also break down and improve the condition of your soil long term. I've used both methods in different beds on our homestead, and we'll still have some weeds come up, but not nearly as many—and they're easier to pull out of the ground.

You'll want to make sure hay has not been treated with herbicides, and avoid using black walnut wood chips. Hay can bring in weed seed; some people prefer to use straw, while others make sure the hay is deep enough so the seeds don't germinate easily.

2. **Lasagna gardening or sheet composting.** This is best done in the fall so the bed will be ready for the following spring and summer crops. The base layer is either cardboard or layers of newspaper (carbon/brown), 4 to 6 inches thick, placed on top of the soil to help prevent weeds from growing up. Wet the layer thoroughly and then add a layer of greens (nitrogen). This is usually grass, though any greens listed from the compost chart on page 117 can work. Now add a layer of browns and then another layer of greens until it's at least 18 inches thick, always ending with a carbon/brown layer on top. Once this has composted down, you can plant directly in the bed, or some people will place compost and soil directly on top and plant immediately.

3. **Boiling water or vinegar.** This works more on spot killing weeds in driveways or walkways or perimeter lines (like fences), not in the regular vegetable garden. Be careful of using vinegar too liberally as it can change the pH of your soil. I wouldn't recommend using it in your garden beds. Oftentimes it will kill the surface of the weed, but the roots will grow back.

4. **Vinegar, salt, soap, and water.** If you hang out in any online gardening group, you'll likely see this from one source or another. The basic "recipe" with slight variations is a gallon vinegar, 1 to 2 cups salt, and 2 to 4 tablespoons soap. Again, this often kills the foliage but not always the root. Both salt and vinegar can negatively change your soil. Don't use this as pest control on your vegetables, you'll kill your plants. Some variations suggest Epsom salt, this is magnesium and won't hurt your soil but has no effect as a weed killer.

5. **Hand torch.** For borders or lots of weeds, we've found burning them to be fast and effective. We use this method along the fence of our vegetable garden, between the plants inside (carefully targeting weed areas only), and along pathways. Use common sense in drought conditions and be aware of general safety. Many gardeners have found this to be an easy weeding technique.

6. **Smothering.** This is slightly different than using mulch, though it works by the same mechanism, using layers of newspaper, cardboard, plastic, and even weed-control fabric. In permanent flower beds we tried the weed-control fabric and found after a few years the weeds just came right up through it. Mulch has worked better for us long term.

7. **Deadhead.** For weeds that spread via seeds (hello, thistles), cut off the tops before they go to seed. We have regular machete thistle head chopping parties in our pasture. This will at least stop new weeds from seeding.

8. **Eat them.** This will obviously depend on the weed, but many things we consider weeds are actually edible. Dandelions, chickweed, purslane, lamb's-quarter, and nettles are thought of as weeds, but they are all edible, and some even have medicinal properties to them. Always make sure you're 100 percent positive a plant is safe for consumption before foraging or eating wild plants; but sometimes, it just takes looking at them in a new way.

9. **Disrupt the surface early.** For bare ground, if you take a hoe or rake and disrupt the surface of the soil when the weeds are just beginning to grow, you can save yourself hours of hand weeding later. About five to seven days after soil has been turned or is bare, you'll see tiny, hairlike weeds just beginning to sprout. If you rake over them, you'll pull out the new little roots without having to individually pull them up.

10. **Goats or pigs.** We've used both to clear brush and, more specifically, blackberry vines. We have invasive blackberries (classified as noxious weeds in our county) that grow everywhere and quickly take over roadsides, fences, and property. While goats will strip the leaves of plants, they don't do anything for the roots. We found pigs to be much more effective at digging up the root of the plant while consuming it and clearing the land. While this won't work for vegetable gardens or plants you want to grow, they can be great at clearing out new areas for a garden or to plant fruit in.

11. **Diligence.** In the spring or before most weeds can really take hold, spending a few minutes each day pulling them out goes a long way come later in the growing season. Not only does it help keep them from spreading, but when they're young, they're easier to pull out.

COMPOSTING 101

Composting requires time. The sooner you start it, the sooner you get to use it, the sooner you'll have healthier soil, and therefore healthier plants. Win!

Composting helps nature speed up the process of decomposing organic matter into soil. When fully composted, it's dark brown, improves your soil structure (especially if you have poor draining soil), and provides nutrients for your plants. The best part is, it's pretty much free and transforms normal yard and kitchen waste into a wonderful soil amendment.

To start a backyard compost pile, you need a balance of carbon (brown) and nitrogen (green) materials with some water. Some people use bins with holes in the bottom for drainage or a store-bought compost tumbler (they're usually black or a dark color to help retain heat, and they rotate for easy turning), but you can also make a pile on the ground. We used some old pallets to create a back and two sides so I could pile the compost high without it falling over.

How to Choose Your Compost Pile Location

I like mine relatively close to the garden and backdoor, making for shorter trips to the compost pile with kitchen scraps. Make sure your hose will reach it, or know you'll need to carry water to the pile during dry weather. Also, a large compost pile can get very hot in certain conditions (this is pretty rare), so make sure it's not near any flammable items to be on the safe side.

If you live in a cooler northern climate, full sun is a good choice (but take care in summer months to check the moisture level). If you live in a hotter climate, you'll want to consider a spot that has afternoon shade.

It's best to have a minimum of 3 x 3 feet up to 5 x 5 feet; any larger than that and it's going to be a lot of work to turn it by hand (trust me, your muscles will thank me). Without having the pile at least 3 x 3 feet, it's difficult for the pile to build up enough heat (heat helps matter to break down and is a sign your compost pile is active) and to retain the heat through colder months.

How to Start Your Compost Pile

To begin a compost pile, you'll use equal brown and green parts. What exactly do I mean by that?

The brown parts (carbon) give energy to the microorganisms that are eating and turning everything into compost for you. The brown ingredients also help absorb moisture and keep adequate air flow.

The green parts (nitrogen) give nutrients and moisture as well as protein so the microorganisms can grow.

It's important to note that when choosing green material to add to your compost pile, you never want to use any diseased plants, and be careful using grass clippings if the yard was sprayed with any type of weed killer, as the finished compost will retain these properties and pass on disease and the chemicals where you use it (aka kill the plants you're so lovingly creating this compost for to begin with).

Composting Parts

Green Items	grass clippings, used coffee grounds, food scraps from the kitchen (vegetable, fruit, and grains), tea bags, fresh manure from approved herbivore animals, green leaves, garden cleanup of disease-free plants
Brown Items	brown leaves, small twigs/sticks (should be ½ inch or smaller in diameter), wood chips, sawdust, brown paper bags, cardboard, newspaper, coffee filters, hay, straw

The first layer should be brown (carbon) items. I create a layer about four to six inches deep, then an equal four- to six-inch-deep layer of greens (nitrogen), another layer of browns, repeating until you've used all your supplies. I prefer to end with a brown layer on a new pile because I know I'll be having kitchen scraps coming out for the next layer each week, and if I get the ratio off, it helps control any smell issues.

For a new pile, I prefer to keep each layer the same depth, with 50 percent browns and 50 percent greens. Some people prefer to go a little bit higher with their green ratio. If your pile starts to stink, you need to up your brown ratio.

As you build your layers for your pile, take a moment to feel each layer. Pick up a handful of material. It should feel damp to the touch but not soaking wet—more like a wrung-out sponge. If it's dry, spray some water on it.

The easiest and most accurate way to monitor your compost pile is by using a compost thermometer and taking its internal temperature. They're less than $20 and will help you gauge what's going on in your pile, when to water, when to turn, and when to add more greens or browns.

I purchased my compost thermometer from ReoTemp and find myself checking the temperature often on a new pile. It's kind of addicting to watch it reach those desired internal temps. Oh, the things only other gardeners understand.

What NOT to Put in Your Compost Pile

You want to avoid manure from animals that eat meat (dogs and cats most notably). They have harmful bacteria for both the compost pile and you.

Fats and meat attract rodents, will smell, and unless your compost pile is at a high temperature, won't break down well.

Dairy items have the same issues as above for fats and meats.

Glossy magazines, shiny, or laminated paper products won't break down well.

Wood chips or shavings from *treated* lumber introduce harmful substances.

Any part (nuts, bark, wood) of a black walnut tree, when using the finished compost on a vegetable garden, can be harmful. Some fruit and berries are sensitive to juglone (a compound in black walnut). Juglone is toxic and fatal to many plants.

Best Practices with Adding Material to Your Pile

Larger items such as paper products, should be shredded or cut up into smaller pieces. The smaller the surface area, the faster the organisms will be able to consume and break it down.

If using hay, remember it contains seeds. Your compost internal temperature should be 140 degrees Fahrenheit or higher to kill the weed seeds (or you'll be planting them wherever you use the compost). Also, make sure any hay or straw you use has not been sprayed with herbicides before adding to your compost pile.

If using horse manure, you'll want to make sure your compost internal temperature is 140 degrees Fahrenheit or higher or you'll have extra things growing where you use your compost.

Internal Temperatures of a Compost Pile

55–70 Degrees Fahrenheit

The *psychrophilic* bacteria work in this lower temperature range. Your compost pile isn't considered very active at this point but these bacteria will help create conditions for the next phase of bacteria to take over.

71–100 Degrees Fahrenheit

The *mesophilic* bacteria are present and active at this range. Congrats! You have an active pile. You've got all the little microorganisms and critters like bugs and worms eating the material in your pile. This temperature is slow and steady for the race to finished compost at six months to a year.

101–130 Degrees Fahrenheit

At 113 degrees *thermophilic* bacteria take over. Your microorganisms are thinking it's a Thanksgiving Day feast in there and are busy turning all those materials into compost. Your pile will turn into finished compost faster at these higher temperatures.

131–160 Degrees Fahrenheit

You're officially hot, and the *thermophilic* bacteria are very active. This is a harder temperature range to reach (usually your pile needs to be 4 x 4 or bigger for this kind of heat) and will usually only stay above the 140 degree mark for two to five days before settling back down to a lower range. Reaching the 135 to 140 degree mark is desirable for killing off any weed seeds or pathogenic organisms that may be in your compost pile.

Remember to keep an eye on things if the pile exceeds the 160 degree mark; it means you need to split the pile and give it a good shower with the possibility that the finished compost is sterile.[6]

When I'm using a large quantity of fresh grass clippings, my pile will reach this temperature for about a week and then falls back down to the 125 degree mark.

When to Turn Your Compost Pile

All the bacteria mentioned above are aerobic bacteria. They need a certain amount of oxygen in order to stay alive and healthy. These aerobic bacteria need oxygen of greater than 5 percent.[7]

Over time, compost needs to be turned. The act of turning puts oxygen back into the pile for the bacteria to stay happy and consuming everything.

While most of us don't have an exact way of measuring the oxygen level in our compost pile, there are a few signs that will let you know when to give it a good turn.

- Compaction: your compost pile has compacted down
- Odor: if it's developing a strong odor, it's a good sign it needs to be turned (in addition to needing more carbon material)
- Temperature: if it falls to 100 degrees Fahrenheit or lower. The temperature fall is your biggest indicator.

If you're using a compost tumbler, turning the pile is relatively self-explanatory. If you have a bin or container, get your shovel to the bottom of the bin and flip the bottom contents to the top, or you can dump it all out onto a tarp (or the ground) and shovel it back in, mixing up the layers as you do.

If you're like me and have a larger pile, it requires a bit more work. But a gardener isn't dissuaded by a little bit of manual labor.

With a larger pile of our size, I've tried to mix it while keeping it inside the walls of the pallets, but I found I couldn't really get all the way to the bottom of the pile. I prefer to transfer it all outside of the pile next to my bin and shovel it back in, adding in new nitrogen or carbon material and wetting down the layers as I go.

Remember, if your pile smells, add carbon material. If there's no odor but a large drop in temperature, add in new nitrogen material. Your pile will tell you what it needs once you learn how to read the signs.

Some people don't add any new material to their pile once it's reached the desired temperature; others, especially if it's a larger pile, will continue to add kitchen scraps to theirs. I continue to add kitchen scraps to mine (if the chickens don't get them first) for the first month or two.

When your compost is finished, add it to your garden, raised beds, and containers and watch your soil thrive.

On the following pages, you'll find two worksheets to help you with your composting.

PEST AND DISEASE RECORD

Depending upon weather conditions and the year, different pests or diseases will be more prevalent than others. One of the best things a gardener can do is to keep records from year to year on what worked and what didn't, always building on successes for a better garden each year.

Symptoms	Pest/Disease	Treatment Used	Results	Weather
Holes and bite marks on cabbage	Cabbage moth	Neem oil	Less damage after 14 days	Unusually cool/ wet spring

COMPOSTING WORKSHEET

Assignment	Answer
Identify possible locations for your compost pile.	
Choose which method you'll use: ☐ Container ☐ Tumbler ☐ Large free-standing pile List supplies needed to purchase.	
What sources do you have available for brown and green materials? List sources you have from your own home and external sources to contact if needed.	

Bringing in the Harvest

❧ SIX ❧

Bringing in
the Harvest

[Jesus] said to his disciples, "The harvest is plentiful but the workers are few. Ask the Lord of the harvest, therefore, to send out workers into his harvest field."

MATTHEW 9:37–38

The harvest is the promise of all your work fulfilled. It's what makes gardeners replant when seeds don't sprout, get up early to weed and water before work, and wash dirt from beneath fingernails multiple times a day.

There's nothing like the flavor or the feeling of picking your own food right outside your back door. But the harvest window isn't always a long one. If you've ever picked zucchini and missed one, you know what I mean. In a few days' time it can go from a slender squash to huge caveman bat.

When bringing in your harvest, it's helpful to know when the food is ripe and the best harvesting tips. After all, you want the produce at its peak of flavor and texture—not too early and not too far over.

WHEN TO HARVEST

How do you know when those plants are ready to be harvested? And when your crop is so bountiful you have more than you can eat fresh, what are the best (and safest) ways to preserve those foods so you can eat the benefits of your work year-round?

Never fear; I've created the chart below for you, followed by written-out steps for specific methods or crop requirements.

Harvest and Preserving Chart

Crop	Harvest Tips	Fresh Volume	Canned	Frozen	Preserving Methods
Apples	Fruit will separate from the branch with an easy twist when ready	1 bushel (42–48 pounds)	12–16 quarts	28–36 pints	Can, dehydrate, root cellar, ferment, freeze
		3 pounds	1 quart	2 pints	
Apricots	Harvest when fruit is yellowish-orange and slightly soft to touch—don't allow to get mushy or overripe	1 bushel (50 pounds)	20–25 quarts	40–50 pints	Can, dehydrate, freeze
		16 pounds	7 quarts	14 pints	
Asparagus	Harvest in spring when spears are 8 inches tall, snap off at soil line	3–4 pounds	1 quart	3 pints	Can, dehydrate, ferment, freeze
Beans, dry (shelled)	Harvest when pods are swollen and lumpy; you'll feel the mature bean inside	5 pounds	7 quarts	14 pints	Can, dehydrate
Beans, snap (green bush or pole)	Harvest when pods are about 4–7 inches (length dependent on variety) and when pod is smooth (not filled out or lumpy with the bean inside) and crisp when snapped or broken in two	1 bushel (30 pounds)	15–20 quarts	30–45 pints	Can, dehydrate, ferment, freeze
		1½–2 pounds	1 quart	2 pints	
Beets	Best harvested when 2½ inches or smaller in diameter. If soil is soft, grasp greens at the base and pull; if compacted, dig roots up. Hold beet in one hand and greens in the other, twist to break off the greens (leave about an inch of top stem to prevent bleeding).	3 pounds	1 quart	2 pints	Can, dehydrate, root cellar, ferment
Berries, general (except strawberries)	After color change, gently tug on the berry; it should pull free easily. If not, it's not quite ripe yet.	24–quart crate	12–18 quarts	32–36 pints	Can, dehydrate, freeze
		5–8 cups	1 quart	2–3 pints	
Blackberries	Gently tug on berry, it should easily come off, if it holds, wait another day or two	12 pounds	7 quarts	14 pints	can, dehydrate, freeze
		1¾ pounds	1 quart	1 quart	

Crop	Harvest Tips	Fresh Volume	Canned	Frozen	Preserving Methods
Blueberries	Wait until berries are blue and fall into your hand when touched, if you have to tug the berry loose wait a few more days	12 pounds	7 quarts	14 pints	can, dehyrdate, freeze
		1¾ pounds	1 quart	1 quart	
Broccoli	Many sources say to harvest in morning while cool. Harvest when heads are firm, before they've begun to swell up or flowered.	1 bushel (23 pounds)		46 pints	Dehydrate, freeze
		1 pound		2 pints	
Brussels Sprouts	Wait until the first frost for best (and sweetest) flavor. Use a sharp knife to cut sprouts from the stalk when they're firm and approximately 1½ to 2 inches in diameter.	1 quart (1½ pounds)	2 pints (may only can if pickled)	2 pints	Freeze, root cellar
Cabbage (fermented sauer-kraut)	Harvest when heads are firm (size depends on variety). Take a knife and cut the head from the stalk at the base. You might get lucky and have a smaller head grow back if you leave plant in the ground.	25 pounds	9 quarts (can only can if first fermented as sauerkraut)	9 quarts	Can (sauerkraut), dehydrate, ferment, freeze, root cellar
Carrots	Pull up from tops; if soil is hard/compacted, loosen with a garden fork first. Trim tops an inch from carrot.	½ bushel (25 pounds)	10 quarts	16-20 pints	Can, dehydrate, ferment, freeze, root cellar,
		2-3 pounds	1 quart	2 pints	
Cauliflower	Cut when heads are tight and compact.	2 medium heads	2 pints (may only can if pickled)	2 pints	Can (pickling), dehydrate, freeze
Celery	Harvest individual stalks from the outside of the plant when they are big enough to your liking (a minimum of 6 inches on outer stalks from the ground to the first set of leaves). Harvest whole plants by cutting at the soil line. Can survive light frost if covered.	1 plant (7–9 stalks)		1 pint	Can (in tested combination recipes, not by itself) , dehydrate, ferment, freeze
Cherries	Fully colored and still firm to touch, taste test	1 quart (2-2½ pounds)	1 quart, unpitted	1 quart, unpitted	Can, deydrate, freeze

Crop	Harvest Tips	Fresh Volume	Canned	Frozen	Preserving Methods
Citrus	Citrus doesn't ripen off the tree; taste test before picking	5–8 lemons = 1 cup juice	You may can grapefruit and oranges as the whole fruit, other citrus such as lime and lemon are used in combination canning recipes	You can freeze citrus whole to use later for zest and juice	Can, dehydrate, freeze, salt preserve
		8–12 limes = 1 cup juice			
		2–4 oranges = 1 cup juice			
Corn, sweet (in husk)	Silk turns brown. Pierce an inner kernel partway down the cob; if juice is milky or white, it's ready. To pick, pull down and twist to break off the stem.	1 bushel (35 pounds)	8–10 quarts	14–17 pints	Can, dehydrate, ferment, freeze
		6–16 ears	1 quart	2 pints	
Cranberry	Two types of harvest: dry and wet. Dry harvest is used primarily for cooking and baking. Wet is used for juices, sauces, and dried.	12 pounds	7 quarts	14 pints	Can, dehydrate, ferment, freeze
Cucumber	Slicing cucumbers are best around 6 inches in length. Burpless cucumbers should be 1½ inches in diameter. Cut or twist off from vine.	1 pound	1 quart (whole pickles)		Can, dehydrate, ferment
Cucumbers (3–5" pickling cukes)	Harvest pickling cucumbers between 3 to 5 inches long, when ridges and bumps are present	1 bushel (48 pounds)	24 quarts	48 pints	Can, dehydrate, ferment
		8 pounds	3 to 4 quarts	7–9 pints	
Dates	Harvest when brown and wrinkled	1 pound		2½ cups pitted	Dehydrate, freeze
Eggplant	When skin is thin and glossy and eggplant is firm to the touch and is large enough size to eat	1 bushel (33–35 pounds)			can (pickled only), dehydrate, freeze
		1 pound	2 pints (may only can if pickled)	4 cups diced	

Crop	Harvest Tips	Fresh Volume	Canned	Frozen	Preserving Methods
Garlic	Harvest approximately 9 months after a fall planting on a dry day. Hardneck garlic is ready when the top three sets of stalk start to brown, softneck is ready when stalks fall over. To pick, loosen dirt with a garden fork and pull up from base of the stalk or dig up. Cure for storage.	12 pounds	5 quarts or 10 pints pickled garlic		Can (pickling), dehydrate, ferment, root cellar
Grapes	Sweeter after a frost. Harvest on a dry day, if possible, for extended shelf life. Grapes do not ripen off the vine; taste test before picking.	1 bushel (44–50 pounds with stems)	16 quarts of juice		Can, dehydrate, freeze
		2 pounds	1 quart (whole grapes)	1 quart	
Greens	Harvest when leaves are between 4 to 8 inches long (older or larger will taste bitter)	1 bushel (18 pounds)	6–9 quarts	8–12 pints	Can, dehydrate, freeze
		3–4 pounds	1 quart	2 pints	
Kale	Harvest when leaves are large enough. Increased flavor after a frost.	4 pounds	1 quart	2 pints	Can, dehydrate, freeze
Leeks	Harvest when stalks are 1 inch across	2 large (1¼ pound)			dehydrate
Lettuce	Harvest leaf varieties when leaves are between 4 to 8 inches long (older or larger will taste bitter)	⅓ pound per head			May dehydrate into a green powder
Nectarines	Ready when skin turns color but fruit is still firm to the touch	11 pounds	4 quarts	9 pints	Can, dehydrate, freeze
		2½ pounds	1 quart	2 pints	
Okra	Harvest when pods are 2 to 3 inches long. Wear gloves and cut stem above cap with a knife.	1 bushel (26–30 pounds)	17 quarts	34 pints	Can, dehydrate, ferment freeze
		1½ pounds	1 quart	3¾ cups frozen	

Crop	Harvest Tips	Fresh Volume	Canned	Frozen	Preserving Methods
Onions, storage	Harvest when stalks fall over on a dry day. Use a garden fork to loosen dirt (careful not to pierce the onion) and pull from base of stalk. Cure for long-term storage.	2 pounds		2 pints	Can (in combination recipes or pickles/ relishes), dehydrate, ferment, root cellar
Parsnip	Best flavor after hard frost. May leave in ground to overwinter. Loosen soil with garden fork and harvest.	1 bushel (50 pounds)	25 quarts	50 pints	Dehydrate, freeze, root cellar
		1 pound (4 medium or 5–6 small)	1 pint	1 pint	
Pea, field	Harvest peas when pods are swollen and you can see/feel the formed pea inside	1 bushel (30 pounds)	6–7 quarts	12–15 pints	Can, dehydrate, freeze
		4–5 pounds	1 quart	2 pints	
Pea, sugar snap	For sugar snap or whole pod eating, pick when pea is slender and young. For shelled peas, wait until pod is swollen and lumpy; shell out mature peas.	1 pound		2 pints	Freeze
Peaches	Changes color and slightly soft to touch	1 bushel (48 pounds)	18–24 quarts	32–48 pints	Can, dehydrate, freeze
		2–2½ pounds	1 quart	2 pints	
Pears	Must be picked early. Pears don't ripen on the tree. Waiting until completely ripe before harvest gives a hard, gritty flesh and the core will rot because they ripen from the inside out.	1 bushel (56 pounds)	20–25 quarts	40–50 pints	Can, dehydrate, freeze
		2–2½ pounds	1 quart	2 pints	
Peppers, hot	May harvest while still green, but both sweet and hot peppers will have more flavor (and spice on hot varieties) when allowed to mature and change color. Twist off at the stem or use a knife.	2 pounds	4 pints	4 pints (⅔ pound = 1 pint frozen)	Can, dehydrate, ferment, freeze

Crop	Harvest Tips	Fresh Volume	Canned	Frozen	Preserving Methods
Peppers, sweet	May harvest while still green, but both sweet and hot peppers will have more flavor when allowed to mature and change color. Twist off at the stem or use a knife.	9 pounds	9 pints (canning for pints only)	9 pints	Can, dehydrate, ferment, freeze
Plums	Harvest when skin color has darkened, are soft, and come off the tree with a slight twisting motion	1 bushel	24–30 quarts		Can, dehydrate, freeze
		2–2½ pounds	1 quart	2 pints	
Potatoes	Can harvest young "new" potatoes by pulling the plant or feeling around in the soil to select harvest and leave the plant. For a mature main crop, wait until the plant dies back and don't water two weeks prior to harvest. Use a broad or garden fork to loosen soil. If you leave some behind, you'll find them in the spring when you're digging up the garden to plant again.	1 bushel (60 pounds)	42 quarts	84 pints	Can, dehydrate, root cellar, freeze
		10 pounds	7 quarts, cubed	14 pints	
Pumpkins	Ready when stem has started to dry and skin begins to harden. For orange varieties, color change from green to orange is another indicator.	one 10-pound pumpkin	4 quarts	9 pints	Can, dehydrate, freeze, root cellar
Rhubarb	Harvest when stalks are 10 to 15 inches long in the spring	1½ pounds	1 quart	4½ cups	Can, dehydrate, freeze
Rutabagas	After a couple hard frosts, pull or dig them up and cut the tops an inch from top of root.	1 bushel (56 pounds)	23 quarts	56 pints	Can, dehydrate, freeze, root cellar
		1 pound	1 pint	2⅔ cups diced	
Squash, summer (pattypan, yellow, zucchini)	Pick when oblong (zucchini) squash are approximately 8 to 12 inches long. For pattypan or circular-shaped squash, pick when 4 to 8 inches big. Check daily, summer squash grow extremely fast. Twist at the stem to remove it from the vine.	1 bushel (40 pounds)	only can in pickled/relish form	26 pints	Can (pickling only), ferment, dehydrate, freeze
		1½ pounds		1 pint	

Crop	Harvest Tips	Fresh Volume	Canned	Frozen	Preserving Methods
Squash, winter (Hubbard, banana, acorn, butternut, buttercup)	Ready when stem has started to dry and skin starts to harden	1 bushel (40 pounds)	16–20 quarts	32–40 pints	Can, dehydrate, freeze, root cellar
		3 pounds	1 quart	2 pints	
Strawberries	Harvest when berries are fully red	24-quart crate	12–16 quarts	38 pints	Can, dehydrate, freeze
		6–8 cups	1 quart	2 pints	
Sweet potatoes	Ready when large enough to harvest or vines/leaves start turning yellow	½ bushel (25 pounds)	10 quarts	20 pints	Can, dehydrate, freeze, root cellar storage
		2–3 pounds	1 quart	2 pints	
Tomatoes	Pick when skin yields slightly to finger pressure or has changed from green to variety color. Note: shoulders are the last part to change color. They will ripen off the vine but best flavor is vine ripened.	1 bushel (53 pounds)	15–20 pints or 10–12 quarts juice	15 pints	Can, dehydrate, ferment, freeze, root cellar for unripe green tomatoes
		2½–3 pounds	1 quart canned	2 pints	
Turnips	Harvest when turnips are 2 to 3 inches in diamter (or younger for the greens)	1 bushel 50 pounds)	25 quarts	50 pints	Root cellar storage
		1 pound	1 pint	1 pint	

Curing Vegetables

You must cure vegetables for long-term storage. This process is not to be confused with salt or meat curing. Below is a chart of vegetables that do best when cured, along with temps, humidity levels, time, and signs for quick reference. After the chart you'll find a detailed explanation of the curing process, along with more tips.

Crop	Temperature	Humidity	Curing Time	Signs Curing Is Finished
Garlic and Onion	68–85 °F (don't exceed 85 °F)	70%	Up to 2 weeks	Outer skins are dry and papery, stems have shrunk and are hard (no green shows when you cut the stems near the neck)
Potato	45–60 °F	85–95%	2 weeks	Small nicks and cuts are hardened
Sweet Potato	80–85 °F	80%	2 weeks	
Winter Squash	80 °F	80–85%	10–14 days	Stem is dry and skin is tougher

Curing allows the outer skin to dry out and harden, making it harder for pathogens or decay to set in. If you're not planning on storing the vegetables and you want to eat them immediately, you can skip the curing process.

If possible, harvest on a dry day at the beginning of a sunny stretch. Here in the Pacific Northwest, I watch the weather carefully to find a long enough stretch come fall.

If you have good-draining soil and dry conditions, you can pull your onions and lay them out in the garden to dry. We never have dry enough conditions for this, so I pull mine and lay them out on old window screens or wire for air flow. *Do not* wash your vegetables when curing. Brush off any large dirt clumps and lay them out in a single layer with good ventilation.

Onion and garlic curing temps should not exceed 85 degrees Fahrenheit, with optimal temps between 68–85°F and 70 percent relative humidity. Temperatures over 90 degrees and direct sunlight can cause sun scald; avoid this. The curing process can take up to two weeks (or longer if temps are cooler and humidity is higher). You know your onions and garlic are cured when the outer skins are dry and papery and the stems have shrunk and are hard (no green shows when you cut the stems near the neck).

Long-term storage for onions and garlic is 32 degrees Fahrenheit (don't let them freeze) with 60 to 70 percent humidity and out of direct sunlight. However, I braid mine and store them in our back pantry with an average of 60 to 65 degrees Fahrenheit, and my garlic lasts a full year.

Potatoes, both sweet and regular, require curing. To help toughen the skins, stop watering a few weeks before harvest. Don't wash, but brush off dirt before curing. If you must wash your potatoes, make sure they dry thoroughly before laying them out to cure.

All varieties of potatoes, except sweet potatoes, are best cured at 45 to 60 degrees Fahrenheit with 85 to 95 percent humidity for two weeks. You'll notice that small nicks and cuts will harden up.

Potatoes should be stored out of the light (or they'll turn green due to chlorophyll, which can mean the presence of solanine, a toxic alkaloid in large amounts) at 40 to 45 degrees Fahrenheit with 90 percent humidity. They'll shrivel up in drier conditions and sprout in warmer conditions. We tried storing ours in our unheated camper trailer, but the fluctuating temperatures and lower humidity resulted in shriveled and sprouted potatoes after three months, with several turned bad.

For sweet potatoes, lay out the tubers (be careful not to bruise or puncture them) and allow them to dry for up to two weeks at 80 to 85 degrees Fahrenheit with 80 percent humidity. The higher the temperature the faster they'll cure, so if temps are lower than 80 degrees, go the full two weeks. The curing time and higher temperatures also help develop the starches and sugars that make sweet potatoes, well, sweet. Store sweet potatoes between 55 to 60 degrees Fahrenheit.

Even if you don't have perfect temperatures for curing, don't worry about it; just do your best. We rarely have a full two weeks of exactly correct temps for onions and garlic in the fall. Erring on the cooler side, simply increase the curing time to three to four weeks.

To cure winter squash, pick when squash is ripe; indicators or ripeness are color change, skin toughening, and a drying stem. When picking, leave about two inches of the stem; this helps prevent oxygen from getting into the squash and improves storage time. Wipe off dirt and dry thoroughly (I will often use a vinegar-dampened towel) and lay in a well-ventilated area at 80 degrees Fahrenheit with the humidity 80 to 85 percent for 10 to 14 days. If you don't have those types of temperatures (come harvest time in September and October we're never this warm), you can cure winter squash in a corner of your house at cooler temps; optimal is around 50 degrees, making sure you turn them over and no rot sets in.

After curing winter squash for two weeks, store in a cool, dry area at around 55 degrees Fahrenheit. I store the majority in my back pantry with a few in the kitchen where the temps are closer to the lower to mid-sixties, and my butternut, acorn, and spaghetti squash last between four and six months. Squash in the cooler part of the house will last six months plus, with our spaghetti squash lasting the longest. Make sure to check them routinely in case one does go bad.

During storage, make sure garlic, onions, potatoes, and sweet potatoes have adequate air flow and aren't exposed to light. I hang up my braids of onions and garlic and store potatoes in mesh bags in our pantry closet. Any containers used to hold potatoes or onions should be breathable; cardboard boxes and paper bags also work well. If using plastic containers, make sure they're not sealed and have a way to breathe or vent.

Never store your potatoes near fruit; the gasses from fruit will cause the potatoes to sprout. It's also not recommended to store your onions and potatoes together.

Check your cured food in storage often. One potato, onion, or garlic starting to rot will quickly spread to the rest. You know the saying, "One bad apple will spoil the barrel"? It applies to these crops as well.

Preserving Crops

Going into harvest time with a plan will help keep your sanity and make sure you're putting to good use all of the food you've grown.

As you've seen from the Harvest and Preserving Chart, there are several ways to preserve most crops based on the equipment you have, preferred method of eating, and storage.

Some methods will require more equipment and know-how than others. The main methods are:

- canning (water bath and pressure)
- dehydration
- freezing
- refrigerating (includes fermentation methods)
- root cellar (cold storage)

Canning involves placing prepared foods in glass jars, processing them in a boiling water bath or pressure canning, to create an anaerobic environment that makes the food shelf stable at room temperature for months. It's important that you understand the science and safety of canning to avoid botulism, a fatal form of food poisoning. Acidic foods that are 4.6 pH level or lower may safely be canned via a water bath (provided you still follow updated recipes—don't use grandma's tomato sauce recipe or older canning books printed on or before 1988 for procedures and times) while other vegetables and meats need to be processed via a pressure canner. I offer a free online home canning safety class that walks you through safe procedures and sets a solid foundation for canning. You can access it at melissaknorris.com/canningclass.

Dehydration involves removing the moisture content from food so it doesn't break down and decay, creating a shelf-stable and lightweight food. You'll be amazed at how a large bowl of fresh cherries turns into a few cups once dehydrated. You can dehydrate food by using an oven, (provided it lets you select a low enough temp) and leaving the door propped open, but a dehydrator that allows you to select the temperature and uses a fan will give you a better outcome.

The freezer can work well for some fruits and vegetables. I will often toss my berries in the freezer during harvest time to later make jams, jellies, and syrups so I can focus on preserving the vegetables that need to be processed at picking time. I'll also use the freezer for vegetables like

zucchini (any summer squash) and greens that aren't good candidates for canning due to safety or texture.

The fridge will hold vegetables and fruits for a few days for fresh use, of course, or until you can get to preserving them using your preferred method. Fermentation of vegetables is one of my favorite ways to preserve because the food is still raw, is teeming with good bacteria for our gut health, and after it's fermented it will stay preserved in the fridge (or a cool environment around 40° F) for months.

Root cellar techniques will allow you to store some fruits and vegetables for many months, even if you don't have a root cellar or basement. Curing improves the shelf life of these vegetables, as we covered in the previous section.

Most gardeners will use several, if not all, of the above methods. We use all of them here on our homestead.

Preserving Supplies Checklist

Canning (water bath)

☐ Large pot with lid or water bath canner with rack

☐ Canning rack (can use extra bands or twisted towel to keep jars up off the bottom of the pot)

☐ Canning jars, lids, and bands

Canning (pressure canning)

☐ Pressure canner with rack (you cannot can in an electric pressure cooker; must be a stove-top pressure canner)

☐ Canning jars, lids, and bands

Canning supplies that are nice to have but not essential:

- Jar lifter
- Headspace measuring tool

Dehydrating

☐ Dehydrator and trays

☐ Mason jars or sealable, air-tight bags

Dehydrating supplies that are nice to have but not essential:

- Silicone nonstick mats or parchment paper for fruit puree, sticky fruit, or small pieces of food
- Vacuum sealer, bags, and mason jar attachment

Freezing

☐ Freezer containers or bags

☐ Steamer basket to blanch some vegetables

☐ Mason jars make excellent freezer containers for many fruits (I freeze quart jars full of berries).

Freezing supplies that are nice to have but not essential:

- Vacuum sealer, bags, and Mason jar attachment

Fermenting

☐ Mason jars or fermenting crock

☐ Airlock system for jars

☐ Fermenting weight (can use a plastic bag or small jar filled with water as a homemade weight)

Root Cellar

☐ Screen or wire to lay crops on during curing

☐ Breathable containers, bags, or bins to store cured vegetables in

HARVEST PRESERVATION WORKSHEET

This worksheet is designed to help you map out your preservation plan, because going in with a plan will help you stay on top of the harvest and have supplies ready. Using the Harvest and Preservation Chart starting on page 131, fill in the worksheet below.

Crop	Harvest Window Based on My Planting Dates	Preservation Method	Yield
green beans	July 8 – September 8	Fermentation and canning	

Perennials: Plant Once, Harvest for Years

SEVEN

Perennials: Plant Once, Harvest for Years

I am the true vine, and my Father is the gardener. He cuts off every branch in me that bears no fruit, while every branch that does bear fruit he prunes so that it will be even more fruitful.

JOHN 15:1-2

We've talked a lot about starting plants from seed each year, direct sowing, and an annual vegetable garden, but we cannot overlook the benefits of adding perennials to your food-producing efforts.

Perennial plants can be the secret weapon to increase food production with less hands-on time. The best part is, you can easily sneak them into your landscaping and yard to get a great return and yield of food without nearly as much work as you'll put into an annual vegetable garden.

Trust me; I'm not knocking or giving up on my annual vegetable garden, but one should definitely make room for both.

Each plant fits into one of three main categories based on its life cycle.

1. **Annual:** This means the plant grows from a seed, produces its fruit, goes to seed, and dies all in one season or year. Most of your summer vegetable crops are annuals like corn, beans, summer and winter squash, and lettuce.

2. **Biennial:** This is a plant that grows and produces leaves the first year, but it doesn't bloom and produce seeds until the second year. The second year you'll get seeds, the plant's way of reproducing, and then the plant dies. This is true of foxglove (not an edible plant—dangerous if eaten as it affects the heart), but also vegetables. Some examples are carrots, celery, garlic, onions, and most of the brassica family (cabbage, brussels sprouts, broccoli, etc.). Many biennial vegetables we eat from on the first year and don't seed save from, and therefore most people treat them as annual.

3. **Perennial.** These are plants that you plant once, and (provided disease or some other malady doesn't befall them) they will live and keep producing flowers or fruit year after year, some living decades or longer when cared for properly. The most common perennial crops are berries, stone fruits, asparagus, rhubarb, and many of your herbs like lavender, mint, oregano, and thyme.

Depending upon climate and growing season, some people can't grow a plant as a perennial (even though technically the plant is one) but have success growing it as an annual. If you live in a cooler climate the frost will kill the plant, whereas in a warmer climate it would continue to grow year-round.

Most gardeners plant all three varieties when it comes to their food production. Perennials are a great addition to your landscaping and your food crops.

PLANTING PERENNIALS

Best Time of Year to Plant Perennials

Late winter and early spring (varies based on snow and when ground is thawed) is the best time to plant most of your fruit trees, bushes, and plants (especially bare-root options). Depending on your weather, you can start planting when you can work the soil (when it's not frozen solid but before everything is completely out of dormancy).

Most local nurseries will begin stocking these varieties when it's suitable to plant them in your area.

Tips for Planting Perennials

When planting your perennial, make sure there's enough space surrounding it to accommodate it for years to come. Every year it will get bigger, and you don't want to have to move your fruit tree in a few years because you planted it too close to something else. It's doable, but you'll stunt the growth and fruit production every time you move it, making you wait even longer for a harvest.

Perennials are permanent, or should be in most cases. Take your time in deciding where to plant them, especially with plants like herbs or strawberries that spread via runners. They can be hard to contain if you don't want them spilling out into other areas. A container or raised bed may be the best option.

If you don't have a yard or area you can plant in the ground, don't think you can't grow perennials. My apartment homesteaders, I'm talking to you. Small and compact varieties of fruit trees and bushes are excellent candidates for larger containers.

Fruit Trees

Fruit trees have three main size types:

Dwarf. This is the smallest and most compact fruit tree. Big surprise, right? They usually grow between 8 to 10 feet tall and wide upon maturity. The size of the fruit is *not* dwarf, just the size of the tree. These varieties may produce fruit sooner than their larger counterparts.

Pros:

- can be grown in containers
- provide fruit in as little as two years
- no ladder or climbing for picking or pruning
- compact size for patios, smaller properties, or even indoors

Cons:

- shorter lifespan of 15 to 25 years versus up to 50 years of a standard variety
- small harvest per tree; because they're smaller, you won't get as large a harvest as semi-dwarf and standard.

Semi-Dwarf. These varieties grow to between 12 to 15 tall and wide (depending on root stock, some may get a few feet taller). Upon maturity you may need a ladder to harvest from the very top of the tree.

Pros:

- can be grown in container
- provide fruit faster than standard variety
- produce double to triple the harvest (depending upon variety) compared to dwarf
- provide some shade

Cons:

- smaller harvest than a standard
- shorter lifespan than a standard
- may require a ladder to reach the top level for harvest and pruning

Standard. These are the big boys. They can reach beyond 25 feet tall on maturity. My parents have apple trees well over 60 years old still producing fruit with very little pruning (they're quite sprawling). Our neighbor has an old standard apple tree that has fallen over in their field and still produces a harvest—pretty impressive for something planted half a lifetime ago.

Pros:

- largest harvest, plenty for fresh eating, preserving, selling, or sharing

- long life span, upwards of 50 years in many cases

- shade tree

Cons:

- take a few years longer to produce a harvest

- require more space per tree. You need some acreage if you plan on having multiple varieties and don't want to plant right up next to your house.

- ladder needed for harvest and pruning

Bare-Root Planting Instructions for Fruit Trees and Bushes

The most common fruit trees and bushes you'll find are bare-root trees, and for good reason. Bare-root trees are your most economical pick and are best planted while the tree is still dormant (no leafing out or flowering). The best time to plant is in the fall, winter (depending upon how frozen your ground is), or early spring.

Container trees can be planted any time of year, but they come at a higher price tag.

Pick an area that receives full sun—at least eight hours of sunlight a day.

Prepare your hole by making it larger than your root system. Dig it a little bit deeper than you need so you can break up the soil, making it soft for the new roots to grow down into. You want to keep the trunk of the tree at its natural line, just above the roots, so don't dig the hole too deep or too shallow. (I end up setting the tree in the hole a few times to determine the proper depth.)

If you're not putting your bare-root tree directly in the ground upon purchasing, soak it in a bucket of water the night before planting. Make sure you keep the roots damp, don't let them dry out before planting, and keep the roots in the shade if possible.

Prepare a cone of dirt in the center of the hole to support the tree and allow the roots to go down the cone into the ground. Remove any damaged or broken roots before putting the tree into the hole. (Same concept when you plant strawberries.)

Fill the hole back in with some dirt about halfway. Add some water. Continue backfilling until you've completely filled the hole.

Now, add more water. The water will help settle the soil and show you where you need to add a bit more soil. Add any soil to areas that need it.

Watering New Trees

When you plant a new tree, it's considered new for the full first year. While the tree is dormant, we don't water it much after the initial watering with planting. (If you live where it's extremely dry, you may want to water occasionally.)

During the first summer, it's important to water your new tree once a week if it has been more than a week or two without rain. I didn't do this one year and lost two trees.

Established trees are generally fine, unless drought conditions set in—then you'll want to give them a bit of water during the drought as well. During our drought last summer, I packed a couple of gallons into each tree once a week. It was the longest recorded drought in history in our area, and all our fruit trees made it!

If you live in a really windy area, you may want to put a stake or metal fence post in the ground beside your tree and tie the tree to the stake to keep it from bending over while the roots become established. We've done this with some smaller, weak trees, but not fruit trees. Generally you won't need to do this, but if you live in an extremely windy area, you should consider it.

Cross-Pollinating and Self-Pollinating Fruits

Many people will wonder why they have a lot of blossoms on their fruit bushes and trees but never receive any fruit. The biggest culprit is they have a cross-pollinating variety without a pollinator. Simply put, it needs another variety of pollen from a blossom of the same fruit family in order to cross-pollinate and fertilize the blossom and form a piece of fruit.

When you have blossoms that never form fruit, it's usually because they were not pollinated.

You need an apple to cross-pollinate another apple, meaning a cherry tree won't pollinate a plum and vice versa. You also need two different varieties that are blooming at the same time. (There are a few varieties that will *not* pollinate another variety; see Common Triploid Apple Varieties chart on page 156.)

When planting fruit trees that do require cross-pollination, it's best to plant them within 50 feet of one another or closer, depending upon the sizes of the trees selected (dwarf, semi, or standard).

I know this sounds complicated at first, but it's really not—I promise. I've done the work for you and created these lists to help you out. You've already discovered your gardening zone and frost dates, right? Good—because some fruits require a certain number of chill hours in order to produce fruit. That means they must have so many hours of a temperature below 45 degrees Fahrenheit during the winter in order to produce blossoms to bear fruit.

If you're borderline on being colder than 45 degrees Fahrenheit during the year, you'll want to look for low-chill varieties (which require less chill time) or avoid growing these fruits.

Fruits that Require Chill Hours[1]

almond	chestnut	gooseberry	peach	quince
apple	cherry	grape	persimmon	strawberry
apricot	currant	kiwi	plum	raspberry
blackberry	fig	mulberry	pomegranate	walnut
blueberry	filbert			

Self-pollinating plants have both the male part (stamen) and the female part (pistil) inside the blossom, so they're able to pollinate themselves without the aid of another variety.

If you're limited on space, you may wish to consider self-pollinated varieties because you'll only need one tree to produce fruit.

Self-Pollinating Fruits (true of most varieties listed)

apricot	grapevines	berries
pomegranate	persimmon	European plum
citrus fruit	sour cherry	peach

Select varieties are self-pollinating, not the species as a whole:

apple	pear

Most berries and European plums will do better if they have another variety to cross-pollinate with.

Fruits that Require Pollinators[2]

apple*	hazelnut	plum
almond	pear	sweet cherry
filbert	pistachio	walnut

*Apple tree varieties are where we get into a bit of a complication. Some apple tree varieties will accept pollination but do not pollinate other trees; these are commonly referred to as "sterile pollen" or correctly known as triploid apples trees (based on their chromosomes).

These varieties are worth having in your orchard, though, because they're some of my favorite apples and are hearty, producing larger apples and larger crops per tree, and they're more disease resistant.

Common Triploid Apple Varieties (cannot pollinate other varieties)

Baldwin	Bramley	Red Gravenstein	Jonagold	Ribston Pippin
Blenheim Orange	Gravenstein	Crispin	King	Winesap

When it comes to pollination, one variety of apple tree works as a pollinator for almost all varieties: the crab apple. That's why you'll commonly find crab apples planted in apple orchards. Many sources recommend white-blossom crab apples as your best bet for pollination.

One reason crab apples are a great pollinator is their bloom time. Their spur blooms open first, followed by the blooms on one-year-old wood, which means you have a longer bloom time window that will match more apple varieties.

While crab apples aren't known for their flavor, they are naturally high in pectin and disease resistant. They make wonderful apple jelly, and my grandmother always added one or two crab apples to her other fruit flavors of jam and jelly as a natural pectin source.

HOW TO CARE FOR PERENNIALS FOR YEARS OF FOOD

Before perennials come out of dormancy for the year (usually late winter/early spring) you want to prune them. Almost all fruit-producing trees and bushes should be pruned.

Fruit trees are usually pruned using one of three methods: a central leader, open center/vase, or modified central leader method.

Central leader: The main trunk grows upright, and branches come out in a scaffold pattern from the center (think Christmas tree, and you've got it!). You'll often see apples and pears done this way.

Open center/vase: Remove the center leader (the center vertical top branch) from the top of tree and shape it to remain open in the center with the fruit-bearing branches coming up from the outside like a vase. Usually apricots, cherries, nectarines, peaches, pears, and plums are pruned to this shape.

Modified central leader: In a combination of both central leader and open center/vase, you leave the central leader until the tree has produced a scaffold of about eight branches, then cut back the central leader and maintain those scaffolds and a more open center. We use modified central leader for the majority of our trees.

If you've been pruning your apple tree to open center even though tradition recommends central leader or modified, don't panic. If the tree is older and established, continue good pruning habits and keep it in the shape it's been pruned too. We have neighbors with a beautiful orchard, and all the apples are pruned to open center/vase. In the same growing area but down the road the apples are pruned to a modified central leader. They both produce well.

It's best to prune your trees rather than be scared you're doing it wrong and do nothing.

General Fruit Tree Pruning Guidelines

- Prune 1/3 of *new growth* each year (and never remove more than a 1/3 of a tree when pruning).

- Remove any diseased or damaged branches.

- Remove any branches growing straight down or straight up (with the weight of foliage and fruit, gravity will cause these to break off or split away from the trunk, leaving it vulnerable to disease and pests).

- Take out any branches that are growing back into the center of the tree or crossing over one another (if they rub together they'll remove the bark and open the tree up to disease and pests).

- Make cuts to encourage fruit bud growth (cut at a 45° angle just above the leaf bud; make sure it's pointing out and away from the trunk so it has space and light to grow).

- Remove select branches from the top and center for air circulation and allow sunlight to reach the fruit in the center and lower canopy of the tree.

- Remove water sprouts/shoots and tree suckers. Water sprouts or water shoots are branches that grow straight up and are new young growth (we leave one to two per tree during the spring so the tree doesn't send out a whole bunch of new ones to replace them all—at least, that's our theory). Tree suckers are new growth usually near the base of the tree and bottom of the trunk, and often beneath the graft on the original root stock. We remove these throughout the year as they appear, not just during winter/spring pruning.

- Never remove fruit spurs; these are short little sticks that grow on older branches (usually more toward the base and bottom of the branch) that have several blossom buds that will develop into fruit.

Horticulture and Dormant Sprays

Horticulture oil smothers the insect and/or eggs. For this method to be effective, you must completely cover all areas of the tree, leaves, nooks, crannies, undersides—the whole shebang. An organic option is neem oil; follow instructions on the bottle for specific dilution rates.

For disease, one needs to know the exact disease in order to use the appropriate spray. Your best bet is your local county agriculture extension office for identification and organic treatments specific to the disease.

Most dormant and horticulture sprays are applied in late winter/early spring. A dry, non-windy day in the morning is best. Make sure no freezing temps are in the forecast.

A home fruit orchard is different from large commercial orchards. Large orchards will use dormant and horticulture sprays routinely each year as common practice to kill insects. But I don't recommend using dormant or horticulture sprays as a precaution, only if needed. I personally have not yet had to use a dormant or horticulture spray and won't unless we have a specific disease or infestation. However, if you have had a large infestation of pests that lay larvae and eggs that winter over, you may wish to use a spray.

Blueberry Planting, Care, and Pruning

Blueberries need full sun for the best production, though they may tolerate some late-afternoon shade. You'll want to pick an area that gets adequate sunlight.

Blueberries are one of the most acid-loving plants around. In fact, our soil is about a 5.5 to 6 on the pH scale and it's not quite acidic enough for the blueberries. Blueberries do best in soil with a pH level between 4.5 and 5.5. My neighbor adds sulfur to her soil. (Refer to our soil testing and amending section in the last chapter of this book to make sure you understand how to do this best for your area and soil.)

If you don't have a large yard, you'll be glad to know that many blueberry varieties grow quite well in containers.

Note: if your soil is extremely alkaline, it's easier to change and maintain the pH level in a container or raised garden bed. Blueberries have a shallow root system, making them a good candidate for containers. They don't like to have their roots in soggy soil; make sure you have adequate drainage.

Mature blueberry plants may reach up to six feet tall, though yearly pruning helps you maintain your desired height. Plant three feet apart for air circulation and keep rows between six to eight feet apart to get lawnmowers or tillers between them if need be.

Some blueberries are self-pollinating, but you will get a larger harvest per bush if you plant two varieties. Blueberries make a wonderful addition to your landscape and can be tucked into flower beds or existing beds easily. Their blossoms in the spring and stunning red foliage come fall make them worth adding to your landscape even without their clusters of sweet blue treats, though, thankfully, one doesn't have to choose.

Smaller bush varieties suited for container planting, or where space is limited, are Patriot, Sunshine Blue, and Top Hat.

Blueberry Pruning. Blueberries are best pruned in the late winter where I live. You want to prune them when the fruit buds are showing but prior to them blossoming; for us, that happens to be mid-January to mid-February. For plants two years and younger, you'll only prune off dead or damaged branches. At three years of age you'll begin pruning using the following steps.

Remove *all the dead branches*. Using pruning shears, snip off the dead branches. Dead branches are dark in color and new growth is red or pink.

You want *the middle of the bush to have good circulation*. If it's too compact, the berries in the

center won't receive much light or ripen well. Look for branches in the middle that don't have much new growth and remove them, these are usually six years old. You'll identify them by larger size, covered in bark, and oftentimes bits of moss; once a branch is six years old, it's best to prune it out. Be sure to *cut the branch off down to the very base of the bush* to encourage healthy new growth.

Identify branches that don't have any new fruit buds. *No point in keeping branches that aren't going to produce any fruit.* Each fruit bud will produce a good handful of berries, so keep branches with multiple fruit buds. Remove branches that grow long and leggy with no branching or fruit buds until the end. Your goal is to keep the branches with lots of new red growth and fruit buds.

As your blueberry bush grows, cut off any small shoots coming up at the very base of the plant to encourage upright growth. It's not much fun to hunch over the whole time you're picking berries. Or maybe that's a sign I'm starting to get old...nah.

After you've pruned your blueberry plant, you'll want to *add new mulch and fertilizer* if needed. We add mulch and a good layer of aged manure. Because this layer is going on top of last year's layer of mulch, I don't worry if it's a little bit hot, as it won't be hitting the roots right away. After the manure I put on a five- to six-inch layer of sawdust. Sawdust or shredded wood of cedar, fir, maple, and pine are all good choices.

The reason we mulch so heavily here is threefold:

1. to prevent new weeds from growing;

2. to help keep in the moisture come drier summer months (though in the Pacific Northwest that's usually not until after July 4);

3. to prevent mummy berry fungus (fungus *Monilinia vaccinia-corymbosi*). If you're in a wetter climate, you've probably heard of the dreaded mummy berry disease—a two-part infection. The first stage is leaf, stem, and blossom blight. The second stage infects the developing berry; instead of ripening, turns into a shriveled, mauve-colored berry that looks mummified. If the infection gets bad, you'll eventually end up with no berry harvest; the infected berries are inedible.

   The fungus comes from a tiny mushroom that comes up the first part of spring (which develops where the mummified berry falls). If you put down a thick enough mulch before the mummies form and develop apothecia (the bowl shaped part of the fungus that produces spores), the fungus can't grow and therefore can't spread.

Raspberry Planting, Care, and Pruning

Raspberries are best planted in late winter or early spring, when they're still in their dormancy, in full sun. Raspberries prefer a soil pH of 5.6 to 6.8, so amend accordingly.

There are two types of raspberries: summer bearing and everbearing.

Everbearing raspberries produce a spring crop and a fall crop.

Summer-bearing raspberries give one crop starting about mid-June through July. I prefer summer-bearing raspberries because most of my other crops are coming on strong August through September, and I have no time to deal with a berry harvest.

Raspberry canes are scratchy and quite dense, so use pruning shears and wear long sleeves and gloves to protect your skin or you'll find hundreds of small scratches on your hands and arms afterwards.

How to Prune Summer-Bearing Raspberries. With summer-bearing plants, fruit is produced on the second-year canes; pruning is required on the canes *after* they've fruited, as they won't produce again.

In the late winter/early spring, cut back the cane all the way to the ground of the spent canes (last year's fruit-bearing canes) with pruning shears. Make a clean cut at a 45° angle at the base of the cane you're removing. Last year's canes are fairly easy to recognize, as they'll have bits of dead, brown leaves and shriveled stems and berries left on them and, if taken care of properly, they'll be tied up to the trellis system. New growth canes have baby leaf buds and are free from your support wires.

How to Prune Everbearing Raspberries. For a spring and fall harvest, carefully cut back the canes that fruited in the spring to the ground, leaving the canes that haven't fruited to produce in the fall. After your fall harvest, cut back only the canes that have fruited (that you've just picked from) to the ground.

For a fall-only harvest, after the canes have fruited in the fall, *cut all the canes* to three inches above the ground. (Some people think a fall-only harvest gives you a larger harvest.)

When you've finished pruning, always remove the pruned canes and debris from your berry area. If left behind, they can bring unwanted pests and disease to your plants. We burn ours; but if there's no disease, you can add them to your compost pile.

How to Trellis Raspberries. You need to trellis or tie up your raspberries. When they leaf out and fruit, they become quite heavy and will fall over into a tangled mess if you don't trellis them. Trellising makes harvest time easier and provides better air flow.

We prefer to place large posts (about five to six feet tall) at the end of each row. If rows are longer than six feet, you may need to provide a smaller post in the center. Take smooth, medium- to heavy-gauge wire and run it from one post to the other (the entire length of your row), placing one strand about one and a half feet above the ground and the other about three and a half feet from the ground. Using twine, tie bunches of four to six canes together to the bottom wire. Then bend the top of this bunch over in a gentle arch and tie it to the top wire. All your berries will be within easy reach come harvest time with this method. This works especially well with summer-bearing raspberries.

Raspberries reproduce by sending out runners. To keep raspberries from spreading, simply mow or cut off the new growth as it sprouts up, usually within a few feet from the existing canes and plant.

To create new raspberry plants, dig up the new shoots and replant in your row or where you'd like to establish new plants. It's best to transplant in the early spring. This is also how you can get starts for free from a friend or neighbor's existing patch, but nursery stock will be certified disease-free.

Our raspberries were from my parents' abandoned raspberry patch. When they moved out of my childhood home, the raspberries were left to themselves, and they quickly became an overgrown mess. We dug up about ten canes to start our own patch.

Berry Growing Chart

Berry	Planting	Spacing	Pruning	Care
Black-berry	Fall or early spring, full sun in good-draining soil, preferred soil pH levels between 5.5 and 7.0	Plant 3 feet apart i 6–7-foot rows with 8 feet between rows	Remove fruiting canes after harvest	Trellis for vining varieties, fertilize in early spring, mulch to help suppress weeds and retain moisture
Blueberry	Late winter or early spring in full sun in good-draining, fertile soil with pH levels between 4.5 and 5.5	Plant 2½–6 feet apart with 6–8 feet between rows, with a cross-pollinating variety nearby for best harvest	1- to 2-year-old plants, remove fruit blossoms and any broken branches in late winter/early spring 3-year-old + bushes prune up to ½ of the bush following guide on page 162	Fertilize in early spring and amend soil for pH level if necessary, mulch heavily to suppress weeds and retain moisture, use netting in late spring to keep birds from berries
Currant	Fall, winter, or early spring in full sun with good-draining, fertile soil with pH levels between 6 and 6.5	Plant 3–5 feet apart with 6–8 feet between rows	Red, white, and pink: cut back canes to 6–8 inches at planting, yearly keep three of 1-, 2- and 3-year-old canes, removing any cane after its third year. Black currant should be cut back above 2 buds (about 2 inches) from the ground at planting time, yearly prune off any diseased or broken canes, or canes older than 3 years old, focusing on keeping the center of the bush open.	In late winter/early spring weed by hand and apply fertilizer and mulch, net in spring to keep birds from berries

Berry	Planting	Spacing	Pruning	Care
Elderberry	Plant in spring in full sun (can tolerate light shade) in fertilized, good-draining, moist soil with a pH levels between 5.5 and 6.5	Plant 6–10 feet apart with a cross-pollinating variety nearby for best harvest	1–2-year-old plants should only have broken or damaged canes/branches removed. Plants older than 2 years should be pruned in late winter/early spring, removing any diseased/broken branches, and removing any branch older than 3 years. Will send up runners; cut and remove to keep plant to preferred size.	In late winter/ early spring apply compost/manure and mulch to help suppress weeds and retain moisture. Water once a week if no rain, especially first year of planting.
Grape	Plant in spring in full sun with good-draining soil with a pH levels between 5.5 and 6.5	Plant 6–8 feet apart, unless a muscadine variety, then plant 12–15 feet apart and with another muscadine variety for cross-pollination	At planting prune back to 1 vine with only 2–3 buds, prune annually in late winter after leaves have fallen and canes are dark brown, cutting down to 4 main vines, leaving a good 10 buds on each. Cut other branches/canes back to just 3 spurs, removing all other growth (grapes are pruned the heaviest of all our fruit; you'll be amazed at their growth each year).	Requires a trellis system. We begin training ours from the first year they're planted.
Raspberry	Plant in late winter/ early spring in full sun with fertile, good-draining soil of pH levels between 5.5 and 6.8	Plant in rows 1½–3 feet apart with 6 feet between rows; apply compost or soil amendment at time of planting	Summer bearing: late winter/early spring, cut back all the way to the ground of the spent canes (last year's fruit-bearing canes) with pruning shears. Everbearing: carefully cut back canes that have fruited in the spring to the ground; leave canes that haven't fruited to produce in the fall. After fall harvest, cut back only the canes that have fruited (that you've just picked from) to the ground. For a fall-only harvest, after the canes have fruited in the fall, cut all the canes to 3 inches above the ground.	Fertilize annually in spring with aged manure and compost, mulch to suppress weeds and retain moisture. Provide a trellis system to keep canes from falling over.
Strawberry	Plant in spring in full sun with loamy, good-draining, fertile soil with pH levels between 5.5 and 6.8. In the center of the hole, form a cone of soil. Arrange the roots around the cone and fill in the hole with soil. Tamp lightly and water. Make sure the plant's crown is at soil level or slightly above.	June-bearing strawberries should be 15–24 inches apart. Everbearing plants 10–18 inches apart. Leave 2 feet between rows.	The first 6 weeks, pinch off *all* blossoms and runners to encourage root development. After 6 weeks, allow each mother plant to grow up to 5 daughter runners, spaced 6–9 inches apart. Clip off any more than this. June-bearing: mow down 1 week after harvest or use shears to cut back to 1 inch above crown. Strawberries are best removed and new beds established every 3 years.	Fertilize after you harvest your berries. Mulch with straw in the fall, allow plants to harden off but mulch before temps reach 20°F. Remove mulch in the spring when you start to see green growth, but keep mulch in center of the aisle in case of last freezes so you can rake mulch back over plants if needed.

Pairing Perennials Together

I'm always up for less work when it comes to food production (let's be honest—any type of production), which is one of the reasons I love our perennials. I plant initially, prune once a year, and then enjoy the fruits of the harvest for decades. No starting seeds in the house each year, no direct sowing and planning around frost dates, no seed saving or remembering to purchase seeds each year…do you see why perennials can be such a beautiful thing?

I also put plants together that like the same type of soil and conditions. Did you pick up on the part I like to make things as easy on myself as possible? Most of our fruit trees are planted together to take advantage of the full sun on that area of our property as well as cross-pollinating.

Blueberries and raspberries prefer acidic soil. Rhubarb also favors acidic soil, so I plant rhubarb between my blueberry plants. Because I'm already amending the soil to make it more acidic for the blueberries, this saves me from having to amend two separate areas.

My raspberries are in a row next to our blueberries. I can cart the wheelbarrow down the center and hit both rows at once when applying compost and manure or when piling in the branches on pruning day.

When you're putting in your perennials, remember to leave room for growth. If you're adding them into your vegetable garden, keep in mind crop rotation and companion planting.

Take care in choosing the planting spot for your perennials. Most of your perennial herbs will sprawl and grow. Within just a few years of planting our oregano, it filled up the flower bed, spilling over onto the deck and invading around the rose bushes. Oregano and my rose bush seem to do quite well together, so though my tale of caution has a happy ending, it is something you want to consider.

When planting, make sure there's room for the plants to grow and they are in a spot you can get into fairly easily to prune and/or divide the plants as they age.

Dividing a perennial is just as it sounds: after several years of growth, usually in fall or early spring, you take a shovel or spade and divide the plant and its roots in half. This gives you an entire other plant and maintains the vigor and health of the existing plant.

Favorite Edible Perennials for Landscaping

One can hardly go wrong with blueberries for landscaping. They have dainty white flowers in the early spring and stunning red leaves in the fall. If you go with a compact variety, they'll sneak into almost any spot of your landscape, including large pots on patios or decks.

Rhubarb is another favorite; with ruby red stalks and green leaves, they make a pretty contrast, especially when planted beneath taller plants at the front of the bed. Mature rhubarb can get larger and spread, so take care to divide every few years if needed for space.

Strawberries have white flowers in spring and red berries in summer, making a cheery addition. They do spread via runners, so put them in a container if you like a manicured garden or bed.

While many herbs can be more invasive, such as lemon balm, mint, oregano, sage, and thyme, they're usually hardy plants (meaning hard to kill) and do extremely well in containers.

Sage has such pretty velvet silver-green foliage. Lemon thyme has a brighter green leaf outlined with white and pinkish blooms; there are variegated varieties as well. Oregano has lots of white blossoms during the summer with a deep green leaf.

Rosemary is a wonderful bush that has delightful blue blossoms in spring. The needles give a nice contrast to other round leaf plants and stay green year-round.

Tuck in a few of these plants to your landscaping or containers for both beauty and food.

FRUIT AND BERRY PLANNING WORKSHEET

This worksheet will be helpful as you add in new varieties or plan out an entire new orchard or berry patch.

What you need to know before planting or purchasing fruit bushes and trees:

- Does the fruit require chill hours (see page 156)?

- Does it need a pollinator or is it self-fertile (see page 156)?

- If two varieties are needed, have you chosen varieties that bloom at the same time and are pollinators for each other?

Fruit Type	Special Requirements	Cross-Pollinator Variety	Planting Location
Elderberry – S. nigra "Samyl"	None	Yes, purchased Sambucus-nigra variegated	Along back patio, southern exposure and hedge along fence line

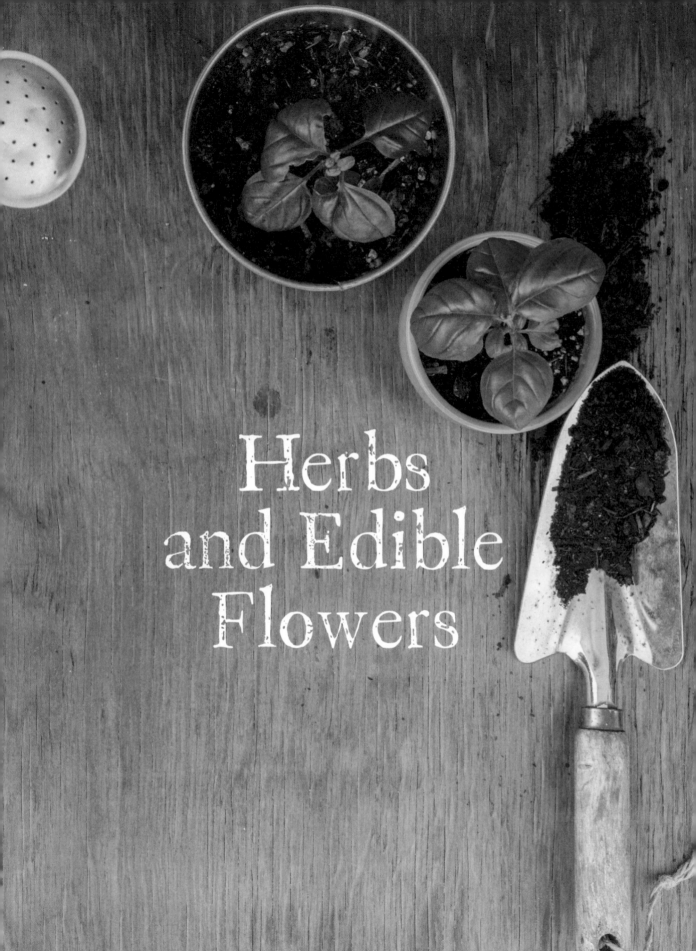

Herbs and Edible Flowers

EIGHT

Herbs and Edible Flowers

Fruit trees of all kinds will grow on both banks of the river. Their leaves will not wither, nor will their fruit fail. Every month they will bear, because the water from the sanctuary flows to them. Their fruit will serve for food and their leaves for healing.

EZEKIEL 47:12

Herbs offer a whole new dimension to the garden. They provide beauty, scent, flavor, and medicine all in one little plant. I feel they're sometimes the unsung hero of the gardening world.

Despite being a fifth-generation homesteader and growing up with a vegetable garden my entire life, herbs weren't something we grew when I was a kid. We had a few flowers here and there, but my mother didn't use herbs much in our cooking and never medicinally.

As I settled into my own gardening routine and began branching out with recipes in the kitchen, I quickly discovered the flavors and nuances a few herbs could bring to a dish. The piney punch of rosemary, brightness of basil, and savory of sage had me eager to try even more herbs, but the price tags at the store…not so much.

If you've ever grown and harvested food fresh from the garden, you know there is no comparing the flavor. Peppers from the store will never have the flavor of ones picked right from the plant. I feel the same way about herbs. There is nothing like fresh basil and chives.

Herbs dried at home seem to have more flavor than dried store-bought counterparts. Even more beautiful, herbs take up relatively little space, can be grown almost anywhere, and truly are some of the easiest plants to grow. Not to mention they have many uses from flavoring our food to gracing our natural medicine cabinets. Pardon me while I gush about them; you'll soon be joining me.

Herbs should most definitely be used in your landscaping and come in both perennial and annual options, meaning there is an herb out there for you no matter what your gardening situation.

One of the best ways to get started with herbs and choosing which herbs to plant first is to go back to your spice cabinet. We'll start with the most common culinary or kitchen herbs and then move into flower and medicinal types.

Many people like to have a dedicated kitchen herb garden close to the house. When simmering a sauce, your mission is to slip out the door, snip off a few herbs, and quickly get them to your waiting dish for a culinary masterpiece. If you have your culinary herbs scattered about the acreage or a good jaunt away from the house, you're less likely to go out and grab them or you're more likely to burn or scorch your dish, neither of which we desire.

PERENNIAL HERBS

Let's start with perennial herbs that will tolerate most climates. Some perennial herbs, especially those in the mint family, are considered invasive. They spread via a runner system and can quickly take over garden beds and spill into yards. For this reason, take care to make sure there's lots of surrounding space for these herbs or plant them in containers. (In the list below, I've marked them with a **CP** for **container plant.**)

Most of the perennial herbs in this list are hardy down to gardening zone 5. We're gardening zone 6 and have had great success with our perennial herbs coming back each year.

The exception to this is rosemary. If you're gardening zone 7 or lower, you'll likely be unable to keep rosemary alive unless you move it to a container or bring it indoors. I've had success with putting it in a large container and keeping it in southern exposure. I've had the same plant for more than six years now.

For colder zones, your perennial herbs will benefit from a mulch layer or straw over the winter months to help protect the roots; however, we've had lows where the temperatures got into the single digits (never negative) and our perennials have always returned, even without mulching.

Most perennials can be planted in the spring or fall.

Perennial Kitchen Herbs (Cold Tolerant)

- bee balm: best in full sun to partial afternoon shade with moist soil **CP**

- chives: does best in full sun, but in hotter climates will tolerate afternoon shade

- horehound: best in full sun and good-draining soil; drought tolerant **CP**

- lemon balm: full sun to partial shade; prefers afternoon shade in hotter climates **CP**

- mint: peppermint and spearmint, full sun to partial shade **CP**

- oregano: best in full sun, but in really hot climates tolerates afternoon shade **CP**

- rosemary: best in full sun (I'm only able to grow my rosemary as a perennial when it's in a container on our southern exposure deck; it always died when in the ground)

- sage: best in full sun; will tolerate some afternoon shade; drought tolerant **CP**

- thyme: best in full sun; drought tolerant; works well as ground cover and in hot, dry climates **CP**

- winter savory: best in full sun and good-draining soil

ANNUAL HERBS

These herbs are generally planted when all danger of frost has passed and will die in the fall when your first frost comes calling. In mild and warm climates, they may act as perennials, but for those of us with visits from Jack Frost, they're annuals.

See the Seed Starting and Planting Chart on page 97 for growing info.

- basil: warm weather only; make sure all danger of frost has passed

- cilantro: tends to self-seed; does better in the cooler part of summer; will go to seed quickly in hot weather, which is your coriander harvest!

- dill: best in full sun with good rich soil; will naturally reseed areas—score!

- marjoram: full sun and good-draining soil; if you live in gardening zones 9 and warmer you can likely grow this as a perennial; for zones 8 and colder, it probably won't survive the winter

- parsley: plant in full sun to part shade; needs moist but good-draining soil

- summer savory: full sun in rich and good-draining soil

Another consideration with your herb planting is making sure you have enough for your preserving needs. All my canners or wannabe food preservers raise your hands.

Below are some of my favorite herbs to grow based on my preserving projects.

Favorite Herbs for Preserving

Salsa Herbs
- Cilantro
- Basil
- Oregano
- Mint (fruit salsas)

Pickling Herbs
- Coriander (the seeds produced from cilantro)
- Dill
- Mustard seed

Spice Mix Herbs
- Basil
- Sage
- Oregano
- Rosemary
- Dill
- Chives
- Summer Savory
- Marjoram
- Thyme

MEDICINAL FLOWERING HERBS

Some herbs double duty as both culinary and medicinal herbs, while some are considered mainly medicinal herbs. These are wonderful additions to your garden because they often add scent and floral beauty.

I used to be a strictly food-production gardener, but over the years I've softened. Not only do medicinal flowering herbs bring a joy to the soul and beauty to the eye, but they help attract bees and other pollinators—a bonus benefit to our food crops. There is room in every garden for beauty and function. Some things are worth having simply because they are pleasing to the eye.

Here is a list of my favorite medicinal flowering herbs.

Arnica. *Arnica montana* is part of the *Asteraceae* (sunflower) family. *Not* for internal use, best in balms and salves for topical use to help aid sore joints, muscles, strains, and bruises. Arnica offers yellow blossoms generally six inches tall.

Growing: Perennial for zones 5 through 9, prefers moist but good-draining soil; it does not like to be waterlogged. Direct sow seed after all danger of frost has passed. Full sun, but in hotter climates consider afternoon shade.

Calendula. *Calendula officinalis* is part of the *Asteraceae* family. Can also be used as a natural food dye, tea, and medicinally is known for its skin-soothing and healing properties.

Growing: Annual, direct sow after all danger of frost has passed in full sun.

Chamomile. *Matricaria chamomilla* (aka German chamomile) is part of the *Asteraceae* family. Commonly used for its analgesic, antiallergenic anti-inflammatory, antimicrobial, and anti-stress properties, as well as wound treatment, a fever-reducing aid, and aid for gastrointestinal issues.[1] Used in herbal tea, infused oils for topical application, poultice, and essential oils.

Growing: Annual, direct sow after all danger of frost has passed in full sun (will tolerate some afternoon shade, especially in hotter climates). May start seed indoors six to eight weeks before last frost date. Prefers good-draining soil; not a heavy feeder; will tolerate moderate drought conditions, but water once a week in prolonged drought or dry spells.

Seed stratification requires seed to go through cold temperatures—either a frost or temps between 34 and 40 degrees Fahrenheit for two to four weeks before germinating in the spring and/or warmer temperatures. The process of seed stratification is nature's way of breaking the dormancy of the seed, signaling winter is over and it's safe to grow.

Home gardeners can place the seed in either the freezer or the fridge, depending on the temperature needs of the specific plant during the stratification period.

Comfrey. *Symphytum officinale* is part of the *Boraginaceae* family. Comfrey contains potentially toxic alkaloids and is not recommended for internal use or on broken skin (don't use on a scrape or open wound). Comfrey is also known as "bone knit" and is traditionally used as a salve or poultice over broken bones or with sprains, joint pain, and muscle pain.

Growing: Cold-hardy perennial; plant in full sun to part shade in good-draining soil. Seed starting requires stratification then direct sow outdoors after all danger of frost has passed and soil temps are above 65° Fahrenheit. May start seeds indoors after stratification process eight weeks before last frost and plant outdoors after all danger of frost has passed. Once established, comfrey is hard to eradicate and will spread; make sure you plant it in a desired location as you'll have an impossible time removing it later. It has a long root, making it a good choice for breaking up the soil, and many like to plant it under their fruit trees as roots pull up nutrients into the leaves of the comfrey; leaves are chopped into a mulch and spread at the base of the tree.

Echinacea (also known as purple coneflower). Medicinal varieties are *E. purpurea*, *E. pallida*, and *E. angustifolia*. All parts can be used medicinally—blossom, leaves, and roots; best known for immune-boosting properties. Roots should be two to three years old before harvesting.

Growing: Perennial; best in full to part sun; needs moist good-draining soil, but will tolerate drought conditions. You can purchase starts or start from seed. Echinacea is one plant that requires seed stratification for best germination rates. For manual seed stratification, echinacea needs both the cold temps of a refrigerator as well as moisture. You can direct sow the seed in either fall or late winter/early spring.

Lavender. *Lavandula* is best known for its strong scent and soothing, calming properties.

Growing: Perennial; drought resistant; full sun; hard to start from seed—best when done as a cutting or start. Lavender does best in poor to moderate fertile soil, and mine grows best in our southern exposure rocky flower bed.

Many home gardeners feel lavender benefits from seed stratification when growing from seed instead of rooting a cutting from an existing plant.

Nasturtium. *Tropaeolum's* leaves and flowers are edible (seeds should not be consumed as they may be toxic); medicinally it shows antimicrobial and anti-inflammatory properties.[2]

Growing: Annual; direct sow from seed when all danger of frost has passed; soaking seeds helps germination rate.

Yarrow. *Achillea* is best known as a wound aid and fever herb. Use with caution for those on blood thinners or with blood clotting disorders, or who are pregnant, or used externally for long periods of time.

Growing: Perennial; start by seed indoors eight to ten weeks before your last frost or direct sow spring through summer in full sun. Yarrow needs good-draining soil and does not like wet feet; well suited for hotter or drier areas of your yard and beds.

Using herbs medicinally is a wonderful thing, but it's also important you understand how they work and any safety precautions. While natural, they do have medicinal properties and can interact with certain medical conditions as well as prescriptions.

Always perform due diligence and research an herb before using medicinally.

BEST WAY TO HARVEST HERBS

Fresh Use

To harvest herbs for fresh use, harvest from the top of the plant; don't just go for the biggest leaves on the bottom. This is especially true for basil. Use a pair of kitchen shears or simply pinch clean with your fingers to remove leaves. Harvest from the top of the plant, pinching or cutting right above a set of leaves to encourage new growth. This also keeps the plant from flowering and going to seed too early in the season.

If basil begins to flower and go to seed, the leaves become bitter as the plant puts all its energy into the forming buds and seeds rather than sending nutrients and growth to the leaves. Even if I wait too long on basil and buds form, I've had good success in encouraging the plant to grow more leaves and avoid bitterness by pinching them off.

Harvesting for Preserving Herbs

For fresh cooking and eating herbs, I harvest any time of day. But for preserving herbs, you want to harvest in the morning before they've flowered or bloomed, when the leaves contain the highest concentration of oils for the highest level of flavor and medicinal properties. I prefer to pluck the leaves from the top of the plant. This helps encourage new growth and a bushier plant instead of a tall, leggy one.

I'll leave two to three inches of the plant remaining so it can continue to grow and produce more throughout the season. If I'm going to dry the herbs the old-fashioned way by hanging, I cut the stalk long enough to tie up.

Most leafy herbs are best harvested before they flower (like basil and herbs in the mint family), but I've harvested leaves even after they blossom, though they're usually not as strong in flavor or can be slightly bitter.

Herbs harvested for their seeds will obviously need to flower and be allowed to go to seed before harvesting. Dill and cilantro are plants we can harvest both the leaves and the seed. I will harvest the leaves all season, allowing the flower heads to mature and do their thing. Harvest seeds when they've changed color and are naturally beginning to dry out.

Herbs used for their roots are generally harvested in the fall, after the first frost. This is especially true for echinacea root. Dandelion root is also recommended to harvest in the fall, because after the plant goes dormant (the blossoms die), it sends all of the energy back into the root.

Herbs harvested for their blossoms, like lavender, chamomile, and echinacea, generally are harvested when the buds just begin to open.

Pruning Perennial Woody Herbs

Your perennial herbs that grow woody stems—think lavender, oregano, rosemary sage, and thyme—benefit from pruning. However, you want to make sure you're not pruning at the wrong time of the year.

During spring and new growth time, remove any dead or damaged branches with a sharp pair of pruning shears. If the plant is too large, you may prune back by one-third. This is when I usually prune back my oregano and rosemary; I tend to be so busy with the other harvests come summer I don't get to the pruning.

During summer, after the plant has flowered, prune back the dead blossoms to help encourage new growth.

Stop pruning four to six weeks before your first average hard frost. This helps the plant go into dormancy and protects it during the cold winter months.

May your herbs provide you with a feast for the mouth as well as the eyes!

HERB GROWING WORKSHEET

Here are a few questions to help decide which herbs to grow based on your family's needs.

Decide which herbs to grow first:

- What herbs are you currently purchasing from the store?

- What herbs do you cook with most?

- What herbs will grow in your growing zone/climate?

Remember to calculate all dates based on your last/first average frost. Some herbs can be started indoors and direct sown; if you do both you'll stagger the blooms and harvest.

Herb	Start Seed Indoors	Direct Sow Date	Transplant Outdoors (remember to harden off)	Source (order online, local nursery, from a friend, etc.)
German Chamomile	March 12	May 7	May 7–14	Seed: local farmer's supply store

Parsley

Advanced
Topics

NINE

Advanced Topics

He who supplies seed to the sower and bread for food will also supply and increase your store of seed and will enlarge the harvest of your righteousness.

2 CORINTHIANS 9:10

Remember when I said gardening is one of the simplest and most complex things there is? This is where we tackle in greater depth some of the complexities of topics like soil testing and amending, crop rotation, and companion planting. Many people garden for years without paying attention to any of these topics and have successful crops.

But most, myself included, find that when trouble arises or crops aren't as prolific as we'd like, it comes down to these three things. Most people's growing issues, and even many diseases, are completely eradicated with soil testing and amendment alone. Hence, we'll cover it first.

Don't let these topics intimidate you. I'll walk you through step-by-step with easy execution plans, but if you can't get to them, don't let that dissuade you from growing your garden now. Okay—let's get to it!

SOIL TESTING AND AMENDING

Getting a soil test done will give you the most accurate results, so you know exactly which soil amendments are needed and how much. Many a gardening woe could be avoided if a simple soil test was performed, not to mention unnecessary work and expense.

Regardless, whether you test your soil or not, your soil will always benefit from a yearly addition of compost. I recommend testing if you're having plant issues or every few years if using the same ground.

Where to Test Your Soil

Most county extension offices will test garden soil for free. Check there first, because we like free.

Unfortunately, my county does not offer this service. After looking at many online soil testing services, Simply Soil Testing won both in price and ease of use; they're local to me but provide this service via mail as well (which means you can use them too!). Contact them at SimplySoilTesting .com.

Testing will vary in price (at the time of writing the full test was under $25). You can choose to only test pH levels or do the full testing on pH, macronutrients, and micronutrients.

When to Test Your Soil

Fall is ideal because you have the winter months to allow the amendments to incorporate into the soil. But you can still test in early spring. You want at least four weeks between making the amendments and planting to allow the soil to absorb the changes you made and make them readily available to the plants.

Your soil results are only going to be as good as your sample.

1. Grab a clean container to put your dirt into. A five-gallon bucket works well.
2. Pick at least six spots evenly spaced over the entire area of your garden. A good rule of thumb is to use a W pattern with equal distance between the spots, taking a sample from each point of the W and one additional spot.
3. Use a spade or shovel to get soil from six to eight inches deep and place this in your container.
4. Place all soil samples into the container and mix together until they're incorporated.
5. Remove one cup of soil into a sealed container. (Or follow the instructions from the soil sampling company; some will tell you to dry out the soil.)
6. Properly label your soil-sample container. If you're doing multiple tests for different gardens or beds, make sure each sample is properly labeled and you retain records on which soil sample goes with each gardening bed.
7. Send off your sample and wait for the results!

How to Amend Your Soil

You've done it! Your tests results are in, but what do they all mean, and how do you amend your soil to get into the optimal range for growing vegetables and fruits?

Your pH level isn't a nutrient but is important for your garden (optimal range is between 6.0 to 7.0 for vegetable gardens). Your pH level should only be amended by one point (lower or higher) over a one-year period. Our pH level tested at 7.09 so I would not want to bring it any lower than a 6.09 in a twelve-month period.

The best organic method to acidify soil is elemental sulfur. Make sure the package says, "certified organic" or "from elemental sulfur." Some soil acidifiers use aluminum sulfide, and I don't want aluminum in the soil I'm growing my vegetables from.

How to Acidify Your Soil

It can take up to one year for the soil to react with the sulfur and show the pH level changes on tests.

Sprinkle the sulfur over your garden soil. Try not to breathe it in and wash your hands after applying; avoid applying on a windy day. (Wear long sleeves and pants and old clothes; it can take multiple washings to get the sulfur smell out of your clothes.)

Work it into the top three inches of the soil.

How to Increase Soil Alkalinity

To increase the alkalinity (lowering acidity in the soil) you can use ground limestone or wood ash. Remember that changing the pH level of the soil is a slow process and it's easier to add more if needed than to go overboard. Limestone should be applied three to six months before you plant and the amount you use is based on the pH level of your soil. There aren't recommended guidelines on how much wood ash per square foot of soil. Most people spread it out in a thin layer and work it into the soil. It's important to test your levels again in the spring so you don't overdo it.

Below are the major macro and micronutrient levels tested. The amount of each amendment you apply will vary based on your tested level, and you should only apply amendments if your soil requires it.

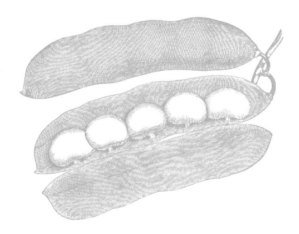

Soil Amendment Chart

Micro/Macronutrients	Amendment Options
Nitrogen (nitrate-N)	blood meal feather meal organic urea milorganite composted animal manure (cattle, poultry, sheep, and horse) Apply 120 days before harvest.
Phosphorus (P2O5)	compost bone meal rock phosphate
Potassium (K)	compost greensand granite dust kelp meal
Calcium (Ca)	ground limestone eggshells
Magnesium (Mg)	Epsom salt dolomitic lime
Boron (B)	compost
Sulfur (S as SO4)	compost elemental sulfur Epsom salt
Zinc	compost manure phosphate rock
Manganese	elemental sulfur compost
Copper	compost liquid seaweed
Iron	compost aged manure greensand

Each element is important for different stages of plant growth and development. When it comes to soil amendment, you only want to amend if that specific level is out of the ideal range.

Soil amending can make a major difference in your crops and harvest, but if done wrong, it can also have negative effects. To access my organic soil amendment guide, go to Familygardenplan .com.

Crop Rotation

Crop rotation is rotating the type of crops (plant families) to different areas of soil to avoid depleting the soil of specific nutrients and decrease disease. Proper crop rotation improves both the health of plants and soil.

It also helps you cut down on the chance of disease entering your soil and endangering your harvest of disease-susceptible plants by separating them out.

Ideally, you do not want to plant the same plant family or plant type in the same soil for at least three years (see list below). This helps the soil rebuild the nutrients specific plants use and cuts back on the chance of disease. Many plants are susceptible to the same pests and diseases; by rotating the crops, you reduce the risk of contamination.

We also want to take advantage of what certain crops will do for the soil and what other crops feed or drain from the soil. For crop rotation to work, we're assuming your soil has been tested and has optimal levels of nutrients to begin with.

4 Main Plant Types for Crop Rotation

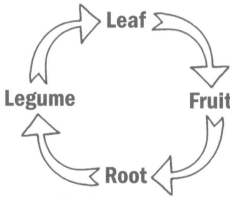

In any given crop plot, rotate in this order:

1. **Leaf.** Brassicas require a lot of nitrogen (cole crops like cabbage, broccoli, kale, and brussels sprouts). Other leafy crops like lettuce, greens, spinach, and herbs are included. While not leaf crops, corn and potatoes are heavy nitrogen feeders, so I include them with the leaf classification for crop rotation. Avoid following potatoes with any member of the *Solanaceae* family as they're susceptible to the same diseases.

2. **Fruit.** Any plant where the blossom turns into the edible crop is considered a fruit. These plants don't need a lot of nitrogen, as too much nitrogen turns into lots of leaves and green growth instead of harvesting and fruit (vegetable) growth. Phosphorus is an important nutrient for bud and root development, but it's not quite as important for root crops (though they do need some). Roots follow fruits in rotation, and because it rhymes, it makes it easier to remember. Crops in this class are cucumbers, eggplant, melons, peppers, summer squash, tomatoes, and winter squash.

3. **Roots.** They don't require much nitrogen or as much phosphorus, which is why they follow the leaf and fruit. They're heavier feeders on potassium, which takes longer to be available in the soil, hence the third position. Crops in this class are anything you dig up to harvest: beets, carrots, garlic, onion, radish, rutabaga, and turnip.

4. **Legumes.** Beans and peas help fix nitrogen back into the soil through their root system. (Contrary to popular belief they don't create nitrogen, but if the *Rhizobium* bacteria is present, their roots have nodules that host *Rhizobium* bacteria and release it into the soil, making it available for other plants to use.) We end the progression with legumes because at this point not much nitrogen is left and legumes will help restore it.

You can follow this rotation at each planting (if you're doing fall, spring, and summer crops) or by year. It works either way. Below is a chart for each crop to help you know where it should fall in this rotation in your garden.

Crop Rotation Chart

Plant Family Name	Crop Rotation Type	Crops	Feeder Type
Apiaceae (*Umbelliferae*; carrot family)	Root	caraway, carrots, celery, chervil, cilantro, dill, fennel, parsley, parsnips	light feeder
Asteraceae (*Compositae*, daisy family, lettuce family)	Leaf	Artichoke, dandelions, endive, lettuce, salsify, sunflower	light to medium feeder
Brassicaceae (*Cruciferae*; brassicas, cole crops, cruciferous crops, mustard family)	Leaf	cabbage, cauliflower, Chinese cabbage, collards, bok choy, broccoli, brussels sprouts, kale, kohlrabi, horseradish, mustard, pak choy, radish, rapeseed, rutabaga, turnips, watercress	heavy feeder—nitrogen, phosphorus, and potassium
Chenopodiaceae (goosefoot family, *beta vulgaris*; beet family)	Root	beets, chard, lamb's-quarter, spinach	heavy feeder—beets especially need boron (they don't process it well), phosphorus, and potassium
Cucurbitaceae (*Cucurbits*; cucumber family, squash family)	Fruit	cucumber, gourds, melons, pumpkin, summer squash, watermelon, winter squash	heavy feeder
Graminae (grains, grass)	Leaf	barley, corn, oats, rye, wheat	heavy feeder—nitrogen
Fabaceae (*Leguminosae*, leguminous crops, legumes; bean, pea or legume family)	Legume	beans, edamame, fava bean, garbanzo bean, hairy vetch, lentils, peanut, peas, soybean	soil builders—help fix nitrogen back into the soil
Liliaceae (lily family); alliums (for members of the Allium genus)	Root	asparagus, chives, garlic, leeks, onions, shallots	light feeder
Solanaceae (Solanaceous crops; potato, tomato, or nightshade family)	Fruit	eggplant, peppers (bell and chili), potatoes, tomatillo, tomatoes	heavy feeder

Many vegetables are heavy feeders, as you can tell from the chart above; but they're not all heavy nitrogen feeders. All plants need a certain amount of basic nutrients in order to grow, but some need a bit more of specific types than others.

While all plants need some nitrogen, phosphorus, and potassium (this is what you see in many fertilizers, or NPK for short) among other core nutrients, others depend more heavily on some of the individual nutrients—hence the crop rotation I've laid out and which many a gardener follows.

I follow some rules more strictly than others with my crop rotation. For example, if I happen to follow a leaf planting with a root instead of a fruit (I plant carrots after my broccoli), I don't freak out or think much of it.

As you gain more experience with your garden, you'll learn what works best for you—which rules you should keep religiously and which ones you bend.

My Hard-and-Fast Crop-Rotation Rules

Never plant anything in the *Solanaceae* family (eggplant, peppers, potato, and tomatoes) in the same soil for at least three years. For example, if you planted potatoes, don't plant tomatoes or anything in that family for at least three more years. This has more to do with avoiding blight than nutrient deficiency. Both early blight (caused by fungus *Alternaria solani*) and late blight (caused by fungi-like mold *Phytophthora infestans*) infect plants in the *Solanaceae* family.

In full disclosure, I have taken a gamble over the past four years and planted my tomatoes in the same soil as the previous year's tomatoes, but that is because it's inside our off-grid greenhouse (or high tunnel) that never receives overhead watering and has never shown any signs of disease or blight. I would *never do this in a regular gardening setting*, but because the soil is always covered and has never had any disease present, I break my own rule.

Never plant brassicas in the same soil for at least three years unless you've planted legumes and tested your nitrogen levels. This was an invaluable tip I learned years ago from an organic farmer with decades of experience.

Plan Your Garden's Crop Rotation

Based on the charts and information above, plan out which crops will go where for this year.

Many people like to draw grids or sketch their gardening areas to plan their crops. I've found it easy to snap a picture each year when the plants are well established (so I can tell at a glance what each crop is) for record keeping and planning the following year's crop rotation.

You may think you'll remember the following year what you have planted where, but trust me—the years start to blend together. Save yourself the headache and document it. You'll find space and worksheets available at the end of this chapter.

COMPANION PLANTING

We've talked about crop rotation, which means we need to revisit its first cousin, companion planting. I purposely discuss companion planting after crop rotation here because I personally focus on crop rotation first and companion planting second.

Companion planting is using plants for specific benefits when planted near other plants. Within companion planting there are several ways to use plants.

If you spend any amount of time on Google, you'll find thousands of articles on companion planting. I tried to look up studies or sources with scientific information, and even then the studies are often conflicting.

Companion planting has been practiced for thousands of years, and gardeners have passed down knowledge of what has worked well with their crops. Studies are wonderful things, but when it comes to gardening, many factors can affect the outcome of a study. I'm not discounting the studies, but merely pointing out there are multiple reasons you'll come across conflicting information, even with the presence of studies.

My best advice is to test companion planting for yourself in your own garden.

Here are several ways to use companion planting in your home vegetable garden.

Trap Crop

This is when you use another plant to trap or pull threats away from your desired harvest crop. Think of it as a sacrificial crop to save the others.

If possible, it is best to plant the trap crop a week or two before your regular crop so the trap crop is established and already trapping pests before the harvest crop is up and producing.

Trap cropping does not mean two crops must be planted together. Sometimes you'll plant a row of a trap crop next to the harvest crop or even between the plants. It may be a perimeter crop. The *Journal of Extension* documented a study where several farmers tried trap cropping and evaluated their results compared to their standard way of farming those crops. In the trap cropping they encircled their fields of summer squash with Blue Hubbard squash as the trap crop. During the growing season the trap crop was sprayed with a foliar insecticide application on several occasions as needed due to rain or increase in beetles.

All six of the farmers said their pest control using the trap crop was improved over previous years. They shared that 19 percent of the squash was damaged by the target pest—the cucumber beetle—and the use of multiple field sprays before use of the trap crop. The results of the trap crop were only a 1 percent loss, and sprays were only used on the trap crop—none on the harvest, lowering their use (and cost) of sprays.[1]

Common Trap Crops

Nasturtiums are another example of trap cropping for pests. Aphids are attracted to nasturtiums instead of other crops. You'll easily see the adult aphids on the flowers and stems and eggs under the leaves. Once spotted, diligently remove them every day. Our preferred method of dispensing with eggs and insect pests is to burn them, but if you can't burn them, place in a sealed garbage bag (make sure it's sealed tight) and dispose of it.

Blue Hubbard squash is a trap crop for squash beetles. The great thing about this method is that if any of your trap crop make it, you have an extra harvest.

There are a few different takes on what to do with the trap crop once it's attracted the pests.

- Spray the trap crop only with the appropriate insecticide (I highly recommend an organic or natural spray if using this method).

- Manual removal—remove the bug manually and dispose of it.

- Nothing—allow the pests to consume the trap crop.

Repellent Plants

Some plants are used as a natural repellent for insects; usually these are your more aromatic herbs and flowers.

When planted with tomatoes, basil is reported to repel thrips and tomato hornworms.

The onion and garlic (*Allium*) family are believed to repel against moths, mites, and aphids.

One of the most plagued crops in my garden from pests are my brassicas (especially broccoli and cabbage). This past year I planted orange nasturtiums with my brussels sprouts and we had our best crop ever. There were small amounts of insect damage, but not as much as years past.

Plants used to help repel common insect pests to brassicas are:[2]

- dill

- orange nasturtium

- rosemary

- chamomile

- sage

- thyme

- mint

We cannot talk about repellent plants without discussing marigolds. The marigold has long been touted as a wonderful repellent plant in the garden. I plant *Calendula officinalis* (commonly known as pot marigold) in our vegetable garden as a repellent, but also for its medicinal flowers and simple beauty.

Varieties of both the French marigold (*Tagetes patula*) and African or Mexican marigold (*Tagetes erecta*) produce biochemicals toxic to root nematodes (nematodes are microscopic worms that feed on the roots of plants). It's important to note: for optimal effect, marigolds need to grow in the soil and then be tilled back in, which allows the release of the chemicals into the dirt; afterward plant your crops in the same soil where you've tilled in the marigolds.[3]

In a study from 1977–1978 in Chesterfield County, Virginia, significantly fewer Mexican bean beetles (*Epilachna varivestis Mulsant*) occurred on beans bordered by French marigold than on non-bordered controls (P <0.01). However, this effect was overshadowed by the allelopathic response of French marigold to beans (P <0.01).[4] In simple terms, they had fewer beetles but noticed the French-marigold–bordered bean plants didn't produce as many beans. One would have to weigh if they had more harvestable beans due to fewer pests even though the crop was smaller and vice versa.

Attracting Crops

Some companion plants increase pollination by attracting more bees, other pollinating insects, and "good" predatory insects.

Good predatory insects prey upon insects that can cause plant harm. For example, ladybugs eat aphids. If you have an aphid problem, adding plants that attract lady bugs is a good use of companion planting. Other insects with good predatory instincts include hover flies, lacewings, ladybird beetles, mantids, robber flies, some spiders, and predatory mites.[5]

Coriander (cilantro), dill, and fennel are all excellent choices to attract predatory insects, specifically hoverflies, lacewings, ladybugs, and parasitic mini wasps.[6]

Not only do these plants attract the good guys, they're also wonderful food crops.

Other crops that attract pollinators (aka bees) and have medicinal and/or culinary benefits include chives (when in bloom), dandelion, echinacea, lavender, and oregano. We use these plants throughout our gardens, and I'm always happy to see the busy bees buzzing about, flitting from flower to flower.

Another benefit of using companion plants is creating a polyculture in your garden. Not only do some plants have repellent or attractant characteristics, but the presence of different types of plants may confuse the bad-guy pests.

Think of it like this: if chocolate chip cookies are your weakness, and you're walking by two tables and one is stacked with nothing but gorgeous plates and platters of chocolate chip cookies and the other table has some brussels sprouts, a cheese platter, and a few chocolate chip cookies, which one are you going to make a beeline for? (Pun totally intended.)

It's the same thing with your garden. If you have plants mixed up instead of one large block of each plant, you're likely to have fewer pests. In the event you do have pests, they're not as likely to spread if you have companion plants between them.

Plus, I think a garden filled with vegetables and flowers is plain pleasing to the eye. Our gardens should be places we enjoy—spots of refuge. Let's make them productive, healthy, and beautiful.

Companion Planting Chart

Plant	Plant Friends (plant nearby)	Plant Enemies (avoid planting nearby)	Insect-Repellent Properties or Beneficial Plants
Asparagus	all—asparagus gets along with everyone	none	
Basil	all—especially tomatoes	none	Repels thrips and tomato hornworms
Bean (bush)	beets, cabbage, carrots, corn, cucumber, peas, potatoes, radishes, strawberries, turnips	allium family (onion, garlic, shallot) reported to stunt growth of bean and legume family	Marigold repels Mexican bean beetles. Nasturtium and rosemary deter beetles. Catnip repels flea beetles.
Bean (pole)	cabbage, carrots, corn, cucumber, peas, potatoes, radishes, strawberries, turnips	allium family (onion, garlic, shallot) reported to stunt growth of bean and legume family, beets	Marigold repels Mexican bean beetles. Nasturtium and rosemary deter beetles. Catnip repels flea beetles.
Beet	bush beans, garlic, lettuce, cabbage family, corn, onions	pole beans, mustard, tomatoes	Garlic repels a number of pests and is thought to improve beet flavor
Brassicas (broccoli, brussels sprouts, cabbage, cauliflower, collard, kale, kohlrabi, mustard, turnips)	beets, garlic, onions	eggplant, peppers, potatoes, and tomatoes	Dill, calendula, chamomile, cilantro, marigold, mint, orange nasturtium, rosemary, sage, thyme, zinnia (Cilantro, dill, thyme, and zinnia attract parasitic wasps that eat cabbage worms and moths.)
Calendula	tomatoes—thought to repel hornworms	none	Thought to repel many pests and excellent pollinator
Carrot	beans, chive, leeks, onions, radishes, tomatoes (Carrots are typically smaller when planted with tomatoes.)	dill, parsnip	Rosemary and sage help deter carrot fly
Celery	beans, brassicas, garlic, leek, onions, tomatoes	corn, potatoes, parsnip	Nasturtium
Chamomile	brassicas, onions	mint (Like most things, mint tends to take over chamomile.)	Attracts good parasitic insects
Chive	brassicas, carrots, garlic, onions, tomatoes	beans or peas	Attracts pollinating insects
Cilantro (Coriander)	brassicas, potatoes	none	Attracts parasitic wasps and repels common pest insects
Corn	beans (pole and bush), beets, peas, potatoes, summer and winter squash	celery, tomatoes (susceptible to same pests)	Marigold to deter beetles in early stage of corn growth
Cucumber	beans (pole and bush), brassicas, celery, corn, lettuce, onions, peas, radishes, tomatoes	potatoes, sage	Dill (attracts good predators), marigold, nasturtium (thought to improve flavor and growth as well as natural pest deterrent)

Plant	Plant Friends (plant nearby)	Plant Enemies (avoid planting nearby)	Insect-Repellent Properties or Beneficial Plants
Dill	brassicas, corn, cucumber, lettuce, onions	carrots, tomatoes	Attracts good predators (I let it self-seed all over my garden)
Eggplant	beans, peas, peppers	none	
Fennel	none		Tends to inhibit growth in all other plants
Garlic	beets, brassicas, celery, lettuce, potatoes, strawberries (I grew it between our strawberries for years), tomatoes	beans, peas	Thought to repel many common garden pests
Lettuce	beans (bush and pole), beets, brassicas, chive, carrots, garlic, radishes, onions, strawberries	none	
Marigold (*Tagetes patula*) and African or Mexican marigold (*Tagetes erecta*)	brassicas		Repels Mexican bean beetles, root nematodes, potato bugs, squash bugs and whitefly. Attracts good predatory insects including hover flies, lacewings, ladybird beetles, mantids, robber flies, some spiders, and predatory mites.
Melon	corn, radishes, squash	potatoes	
Nasturtium	brassicas, melons, radishes, potatoes, squash, tomatoes		Repels whiteflies and beetles and is an excellent pollinator; trap crop for aphids
Onion	beets, brassicas, carrots, lettuce, peppers, strawberries, tomatoes	beans, peas	Deters maggots
Oregano	asparagus, brassicas	none	Repels cabbage moths but is best planted in pots; it takes over beds.
Parsley	asparagus, corn, tomatoes	garlic, mint, onions	Blooms attract good predatory insects
Pea	beans (bush and pole), carrots, celery, cucumber, corn, peppers, potatoes, radishes, spinach, strawberries, turnips	garlic, leeks, onions, shallots	
Pepper	asparagus, basil, carrots, cucumber, eggplant, squash, tomatoes	beans, brassicas	
Potato	basil, beans (bush and pole), brassicas, corn, eggplant, garlic, peas, onions	carrots, squash, tomatoes	Basil repels potato beetles and marigold deter nematodes
Radish	beans (bush and pole), beets, eggplant, lettuce, melons, peas, spinach, squash, tomatoes	brussels sprouts, potatoes, turnips	

Plant	Plant Friends (plant nearby)	Plant Enemies (avoid planting nearby)	Insect-Repellent Properties or Beneficial Plants
Rosemary	brassicas, beans, carrots, sage	tomatoes	Repels cabbage moth, carrot rust fly, and Mexican bean beetle
Sage	brassicas, beans (bush and pole), carrots, strawberries, tomatoes	basil, cucumbers, onions	Sage deters cabbage moth and carrot rust fly but will spread; consider using in containers
Spinach	brassica, beans (bush and pole), peas, strawberries	none	
Squash (summer and winter)	beans (bush and pole), corn, lettuce, marigolds, melons, nasturtium, okra, radishes	brassicas, potatoes	Marigold deters beetles, nasturtium deters beetles and squash bugs, and oregano deters common pests
Strawberry	bush beans, lettuce, onions, spinach, thyme	brassicas, eggplant, melons, okra, peppers, potatoes, tomatoes	Thyme is thought to increase crop yield and deter worms
Summer savory	brassicas, garlic, onions		Repels cabbage moth
Thyme	brassicas	none	Deters cabbage moth, but will spread; consider using a container
Tomato	asparagus, basil, beans (bush and pole), brassicas, carrots, celery, cucumbers, eggplant, garlic, onions, parsley, peppers	corn, dill, kohlrabi (can effect tomato growth), potatoes	Basil helps repel flies and is thought to increase flavor. Calendula deters worms and marigold deters nematodes.
Turnip	brassicas, peas	carrots, potatoes, and radishes	

CROP ROTATION PLANNING

You'll notice in my personal crop rotation and companion planting garden sketch below that my crops don't follow a perfect crop rotation. For example, in my Year 1 plot I have garlic (a root crop) and in Year 2 it is followed by zucchini (a fruit crop), which is "backward" to the standard crop rotation. I don't worry as much about swapping out root and fruit order. But I do make sure my brassicas each year are grown in different spots and follow directly behind the green beans (legumes).

You may notice that a few onion plants are close to the green pole beans in Year 1 and in Year 2 my dill is next to my carrots. I did not notice any difference in the production of the green beans or the carrots and dill. I try to follow these rules as guidelines, but I don't stress about it if I need to break a few of the rules to get all my crops in the ground. I do take notes to see if there are any negative effects when I break a rule, and as I shared previously, never break the rule of planting brassicas in the same soil as nightshade family vegetables.

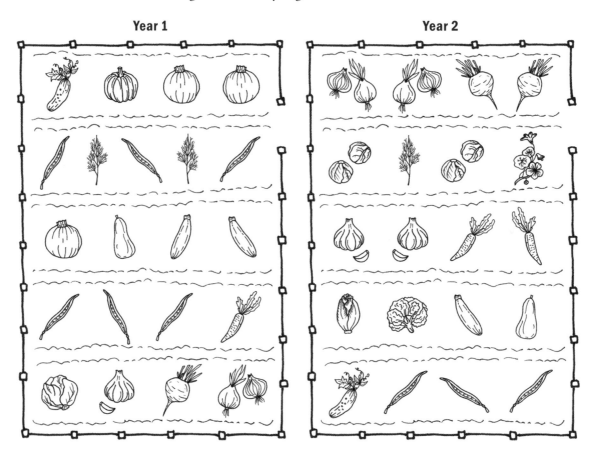

Year 1 Year 2

Crop Rotation

Take an opportunity to plan and sketch out your garden plan keeping in mind these advanced topics like crop rotation, companion planting, etc!

Year 1

Year 2

Year 3

Conclusion

Oh, my friend, I'm so thrilled you've made it all the way through this book. The things you will grow, the lessons you'll learn, and the food, oh the food, you will eat. A garden truly is an ever-producing miracle.

This isn't a one-time read through. The charts and information within these pages will serve you for seasons and years to come. Just as this book will help you for years on end, I would love to help you for years on end.

There's something so important about having a community of others who understand your glee at harvesting your first carrot of the year or your first fruit from your own bushes, and comfort you when you lose a plant (because it happens, even to the best of us). I would be honored and thrilled to have you join me and my community (because frankly, Pioneering Today readers are the best there are). So go get yourself signed up for all the awesome bonuses and continuing information to help you create your best-producing garden ever at familygardenplan.com.

THE GROW CHALLENGE

No matter how many books or articles you read, there's only one way to grow your own food: you must put seeds or plants in the ground and begin.

Over time, you will discover what works best for you and your garden. Some things will evolve and change over time, while others will be mainstays in your growing. You will be amazed at the flavors of home-grown produce and the satisfaction you feel that can never compare with purchasing the same food from a grocery store.

You will also run into frustrations. It is the nature of nature. But I've created videos and bonuses to help you overcome and even bypass many a common frustration.

The best news is, they are yours for *free* with your purchase of this book. To access them, go to familygardenplan.com.

NOTES

Chapter 1

1. Lucy Bradley, "Frost Protection," University of Arizona Tuscon, April 1998, https://extension.arizona.edu/sites/extension.arizona.edu/files/pubs/az1002.pdf.

Chapter 2

1. Linda Chalker-Scott, PhD, "The Myth of Allelopathic Wood Chips," Washington State University Puyallup Research and Extension Center, (n.d.), https://s3.wp.wsu.edu/uploads/sites/403/2015/03/aleopathic-wood-chips.pdf.

2. Washington State University Master Gardener Program, "Container Vegetable Gardening," (n.d.), https://s3.wp.wsu.edu/uploads/sites/2088/2017/04/Container-Vegetable-Gardening_RS004-2010.pdf.

3. Richard Evans, "The Development and Properties of Container Soils—Making a Good Mix," Cooperative Extension Specialist Department of Environmental Horticulture, University of California, Davis, https://ucanr.edu/sites/EH_RIC/newsletters/Vol2_No1_Winter_199837629.pdf.

4. Kathleen M. Kelley, James C. Sellmer, Phyllis Lamont, "Homemade Potting Media," Pennsylvania State University, October 22, 2007, https://extension.psu.edu/homemade-potting-media.

Chapter 3

1. C.W. Schmidt, "Natural born killers," November 1998, https://www.ncbi.nlm.nih.gov/pubmed/9721262.

2. United States Department of Agriculture, "Adoption of Genetically Engineered Crops in the U.S.," July 16, 2018, https://www.ers.usda.gov/data-products/adoption-of-genetically-engineered-crops-in-the-us/recent-trends-in-ge-adoption.aspx.

Chapter 4

1. Jim Sellmer, PhD, and Kathy Kelley, PhD, "How to Pasteurize Medium and Sterilize Containers and Tools," Pennsylvania State University Department of Horticulture Fact Sheet, October 22, 2007, https://extension.psu.edu/how-to-pasteurize-medium-and-sterilize-containers-and-tools.

Chapter 5

1. Suman Chaudhary, Rupinder K. Kanwar, Alka Sehgal, David M. Cahill, Colin J. Barrow, Rakesh Sehgal, and Jagat R. Kanwar "Progress on *Azadirachta indica* Based Biopesticides in Replacing Synthetic Toxic Pesticides," *Frontiers in Plant Science* 8 (May 2017): 610, https://www.ncbi.nlm.nih.gov/pmc/articles/PMC5420583/.

2. S. Newman and L.P. Pottorff, "Powdery Mildew vs Downy Mildew," University of Florida Gardening Solutions (n.d.), http://gardeningsolutions.ifas.ufl.edu/care/pests-and-diseases/diseases/powdery-vs-downy.html.

3. Peter Crisp, "Mode of action of milk and whey in the control of grapevine powdery mildew," *Australasian Plant Pathology* 35 (2006): 487493, https://www.researchgate.net/publication/237377262_Mode_of_action_of_milk_and_whey_in_the_control_of_grapevine_powdery_mildew.

4. Christoph Then, Andreas Bauer-Panskus, "Possible health impacts of Bt toxins and residues from spraying with complementary herbicides in genetically engineered soybeans and risk assessment as performed by the European Food Safety Authority EFS," *Environmental Sciences Europe* 29, no. 1 (2017): 1, https://www.ncbi.nlm.nih.gov/pmc/articles/PMC5236067/.

5. Abby Seaman, "Biology and Management of Squash Vine Borer in Organic Farming Systems," New York State Integrated Pest Management Program, Cornell University, August 14, 2018, https://articles.extension.org/pages/65684/biology-and-management-of-squash-vine-borer-in-organic-farming-systems.

6. University of Illinois Extension, "Composting for the Homeowner," University of Illinois Board of Trust-ees, copyright 2019, https://m.extension.illinois.edu/homecompost/science.cfm.

7. Ibid.

Chapter 7

1. Raintree Nursery, "Chill Hours," https://raintreenursery.com/chill_hours.

2. Robert Crassweller, "Pollination Requirements for Various Fruits and Nuts," PennState Extension, June 9, 2016, https://extension.psu.edu/pollination-requirements-for-various-fruits-and-nuts.

Chapter 8

1. Ompal Singh, Zakia Khanam, Neelam Misra, Manoj Kumar Srivastava, "Chamomile (*Matricaria chamomilla* L.): An Overview," *Pharmacognosy Review* 5, no. 9 (January–June 2011): 82–95, https://www.ncbi.nlm.nih.gov/pmc/articles/PMC3210003/.

2. Monica Butnariu and Cristian Bostan, "Antimicrobial and anti-inflammatory activities of the volatile oil compounds from *Tropaeolum majus* L. (Nasturtium)," *African Journal of Biotechnology* 10, no. 31 (June 2011): 59005905, https://academicjournals.org/article/article1380902607_Butnariu%20and%20Bostan.pdf.

Chapter 9

1. T. Jude Boucher and Robert Durgy, "Demonstrating a Perimeter Trap Crop Approach to Pest Management on Summer Squash in New England," *Journal of Extension* 42, no. 5 (October 2004): https://www.joe.org/joe/2004october/rb2.php.

2. Joyce E. Parker, William E. Snyder, George C. Hamilton, and Cesar Rodriguez Saona, "Companion Planting and Insect Pest Control," https://www.intechopen.com/books/weed-and-pest-control-conventional-and-new-challenges/companion-planting-and-insect-pest-control.

3. UMass Extension Center for Agriculture, "Companion Planting in the Vegetable Garden," (n.d.), https://ag.umass.edu/sites/ag.umass.edu/files/fact-sheets/pdf/companion_planting.pdf.

4. M. A. Latheef, and R. D. Irwin, "Effects of Companionate Planting on Snap Bean Insects, *Epilachna varivestia* and *Heliothis zed*," *Environmental Entomology* 9, no. 2 (April 1980): 195198, https://academic.oup.com/ee/article-abstract/9/2/195/2366695?redirectedFrom=fulltext.

5. George Kuepper, and Mardi Dodson, "Companion Planting and Botanical Pesticides: Concepts and Resources," ATTRA Sustainable Agriculture, updated April 2016 by Justin Duncan, https://attra.ncat.org/viewhtml/?id=72#scientific.

6. Fred Hoffman "Plants that Attract Beneficial Insects," Permaculture Research Institute, October 4, 2014, https://permaculturenews.org/2014/10/04/plants-attract-beneficial-insects/.

INDEX

ABOUT THE AUTHOR

Melissa K. Norris helps hundreds of thousands of people each month to raise their own food and create a homemade and home-grown kitchen, home, garden, and barnyard through her website, popular Pioneering Today podcast, the Pioneering Today Academy, and her books.

Melissa lives with her husband and two kids in their own little house in the big woods in the foothills of the North Cascade Mountains. When she's not playing in the garden, you can find her stuffing food into mason jars (after washing her hands, of course), or creating something delicious in a cast-iron skillet and sharing it with others.

To make sure you're one of those people she's sharing it with along with other resources, subscribe to her free e-mail newsletter by visiting **MelissaKNorris.com**

Scripture quotations are taken from the Holy Bible, New International Version®, NIV®.
Copyright © 1973, 1978, 1984, 2011 by Biblica, Inc. ® Used by permission. All rights reserved world-wide. Published in association with WordServe Literary Group, Ltd., www.wordserveliterary.com.

Cover photo and interior photography by Jay Eads
Cover and interior design by Dugan Design Group
Cover illustration © ziivvn/Fotolia
Interior illustrations © Brigantine Designs/Mighty Deals

The Family Garden Plan

Copyright © 2020 by Melissa K. Norris
Published by Harvest House Publishers
Eugene, Oregon 97408
www.harvesthousepublishers.com

ISBN 978-0-7369-7761-6 (pbk)
ISBN 978-0-7369-7762-3 (eBook)

Library of Congress Cataloging-in-Publication Data Record is available at
https://lccn.lbc.gov/2019016412

Printed in the United States of America

20 21 22 23 24 25 26 27/ VP—DDG / 10 9 8 7 6 5 4 3